THE FRENCH TRAVELMATE

compiled by
LEXUS

RICHARD DREW PUBLISHING
Glasgow

RICHARD DREW PUBLISHING LTD.
6 CLAIRMONT GARDENS
GLASGOW G3 7LW
SCOTLAND

First Published 1982
First Reprint April 1982
Second Reprint May 1984
Third Reprint May 1985
New Edition 1988
Reprinted 1989
Reprinted 1990

ISBN 0 86267 209 0

Printed and bound in Great Britain by
Cox & Wyman Ltd.

YOUR TRAVELMATE gives you one single A–Z list of useful words and phrases to help you communicate in French. Built into this list are travel tips, with facts and figures which provide valuable information; French words you'll see on signs and notices; and typical replies to some of the things you might want to say. There is a menu reader on pp. 72–73, and numbers are given on the last page.

Your TRAVELMATE also tells you how to pronounce French. Just read the pronunciations as though they were English, and you will communicate – although you might not sound like a native speaker. The typical French nasal sounds are represented by [ōn] and [ān]. [j] is like the second consonant sound in 'measure' or 'seizure'. Practice and listening to the French will soon help you distinguish between difficult sounds.

Depending on the likely context of use, the TRAVELMATE gives the French equivalent of either 'the' or 'a'. In some cases, you will also find 'du', 'de la' or plural 'des', for English 'some'. The feminine form of adjectives has not, as a rule, been given; remember that the final consonant is sounded in the feminine form: chaud, chaude [shoh, shohd], creux, creuse [krer, krerz], certain, certaine [sair-tān, sair-ten]

The present tense of verbs will be sufficient to help you get by in most situations:
arriver [ahree-vay] – j'arrive [jah-reev], tu arrives [too ah-reev], il (elle) arrive [eel, el ah-reev], nous arrivons [nooz ahree-von], vous arrivez [vooz ahree-vay], ils (elles) arrivent [eelz, elz ah-reev]

Finally, you may need to spell your name:
a [ah] b [bay] c [say] d [day] e [ay] f [eff] g [jay]
h [ash] i [ee] j [jee] k [kah] l [el] m [em] n [en] o [oh]
p [pay] q [koo] r [airr] s [ess] t [tay] u [oo] v [vay]
w [doobler vay] x [eeks] y [ee-grek] z [zed]

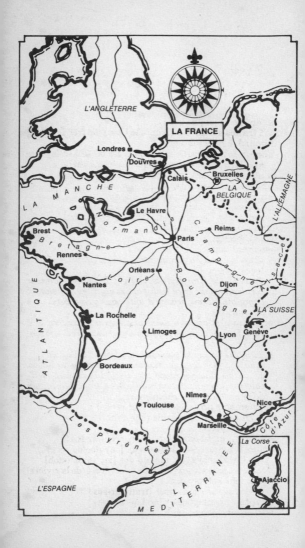

a, an un (une) [ān, oon]
    5 francs a litre cinq francs le litre [sān frōn ler leetr]
aboard à bord [ah-bor]
about: is he about? est-ce qu'il est là? [eskee-lay lah]
    about 15 environ quinze [ōnvee-rōn kānz]
    about 2 o'clock vers deux heures [vair . . .]
above: au-dessus (de . . .) [oh der-soo]
abroad à l'étranger [ah laytrōn-jay]
absolutely absolument [apsoh-loo-mōn]
accelerator l'accélérateur [axay-lay-rah-terr]
accept accepter [axep-tay]
accès interdit *no entry*
accident un accident [axee-dōn]
    there's been an accident il y a eu un accident
    [eelyah oo . . .]
» *TRAVEL TIP: if anybody is hurt, get the police; for minor*
   accidents, make sure both parties sign the 'constat à
   l'amiable' (forms provided with your green card
   documents)
accommodation: we need accommodation for 3 il
    nous faut de la place pour trois personnes [eel noo foh
    der lah plass . . .]
» *TRAVEL TIP: go to the local 'syndicat d'initiative'*
   (tourist office) for information; one- or two-star hotels
   are almost always a good bet; also 'gîtes ruraux' (self-
   catering accommodation) and 'gîtes d'étape' (dormitory
   accommodation for ramblers etc)
accotements non stabilisés *soft verges*
accountant un comptable [kōn-tahbl]
accurate précis
A.C.F. = *Automobile Club de France, like RAC*
ache: it aches c'est douloureux [say dooloo-rer]
    my back aches j'ai mal au dos [jay maloh-doh]
across: across (the river) de l'autre côté (de la rivière)
    [der loht koh-tay der . . .]
    to get across traverser [trahvair-say]
adaptor un adaptateur [ahdap-tah-terr]
add ajouter [ahjoo-tay]

....

address une adresse [ah-dress]
  will you give me your address? est-ce que vous
  pouvez me donner votre adresse? [esker voo poovay
  mer doh-nay . . .]
adjust ajuster [ahjoos-tay]
admission *(to disco etc)* l'entrée [ōn-tray]
advance: can we book in advance? est-ce qu'on peut
  réserver à l'avance? [eskōn per rayzair-vay ah
  lah-vōns]
advert une annonce [ah-nōns]
afraid: I'm afraid I don't know je regrette, je ne sais
  pas [jer rer-gret . . .]
  he's afraid of . . . il a peur de . . . [eel ah per der]
after après [ah-pray]
  after you après vous
afternoon l'après-midi [ahpray-mee-dee]
  in the afternoon l'après-midi
aftershave un aftershave
again de nouveau [noo-voh]
against contre [kōntr]
age l'âge [ahj]
  under age mineur [mee-nerr]
  ages très longtemps [tray lōn-tōn]
agent un représentant [rerpray-sōn-tōn]
ago: a week ago il y a une semaine [eelyah . . .]
  it wasn't long ago il n'y a pas longtemps
  [eelnyah-pah . . .]
  how long ago? il y a combien de temps?
  [kōnb-yān . . .]
agree: I agree je suis d'accord [jer swee dah-kor]
  it doesn't agree with me ça ne me convient pas [san
  mer kōnv-yān pah]
air l'air
  by air en avion [ānn ahv-yōn]
  by air mail par avion
  with air-conditioning climatisé [kleemah-tee-zay]
airport l'aéroport [ah-ayroh-por]
alarm: give the alarm donnez l'alarme
  alarm clock un réveil [ray-vay]
alcohol l'alcool [al-kol]
  is it alcoholic? est-ce que c'est alcoolisé?
  [. . . alkolee-zay]
alimentation food

alive vivant [vee-vȯn]
  is he still alive? est-ce qu'il vit encore?
all *(everything)* tout [too]
  (everybody) tous (toutes) [toos, toot]
  it's all right, I'm all right ça va [sah vah]
  all right! d'accord! [dah-kor]
  that's all c'est tout [say-too]
  thank you, not at all merci, de rien [mairsee der ree-yȧn]
  all night toute la nuit, all day toute la journée
  all I have/want tout ce que j'ai/je veux [toos-ker . . .]
allergic: I'm allergic to . . . je suis allergique à . . . [jer swee ahlair-jeek]
allowed: is it allowed? est-ce que c'est permis? [eskersay pair-mee]
  allow me . . . permettez-moi . . .
allumez vos phares *headlights on*
almost presque [presk]
alone seul [serl]
  did you come here alone? est-ce que vous êtes venu ici tout seul? [esker voo zait ver-noo . . .]
  leave me alone! laissez-moi tranquille! [laysay mwah trȯn-keel]
already déjà [day-jah]
also aussi [oh-see]
although bien que [bee-yȧn ker]
altogether ensemble [ȯn-sȯnbl]
  what does that make altogether? qu'est-ce que ça fait au total? [kesker sah fay oh toh-tal]
always toujours [too-joor]
a.m.: 10 a.m. dix heures du matin [. . . doo mah-tȧn]
ambassador l'ambassadeur [ȯnbah-sah-derr]
ambulance l'ambulance [ȯnboo-lȯns]
  get an ambulance! appelez une ambulance!
» *TRAVEL TIP: no central number; in an emergency ring 'Police Secours'*
America l'Amérique [ahmay-rik]
  American américain [ahmay-ree-kȧn]
among parmi [. . . mee]
amp ampère [ȯn-pair]
  15 amp fuse un fusible de 15 ampères [foo-zeebl . . .]

....

anchor l'ancre [oñkr]

and et [ay]

angry fâché [fah-shay]

   don't get angry ne vous fâchez pas [ner voo fah-shay pah]

ankle la cheville [sher-vee]

anniversary: it's our anniversary c'est notre anniversaire de mariage [ahnee-vair-sair der mahr-yahj]

annoy: he's annoying me il m'importune [añpor-toon]

   it's very annoying c'est très ennuyeux [oñ-nwee-yer]

anorak un anorak

another: can we have another room? est-ce qu'on peut avoir une autre chambre? [eskoñ per ah-vwahr oon-ohtr . . .]

   another beer, please encore une bière, s'il vous plaît

answer une réponse [ray-poñs]

   to answer répondre

   there's no answer on ne répond pas

antifreeze l'antigel [oñtee-jel]

any: have you got any bread/water? est-ce que vous avez du pain/de l'eau? [. . . doo pañ, der loh]

   have you got any rooms? est-ce que vous avez des chambres? [. . . day shoñbr]

   we haven't got any money/tickets nous n'avons pas d'argent/de billets [. . . dahr-joñ, der bee-yay]

   I haven't got any je n'en ai pas [jer noñn ay pah]

anybody: is anybody there? est-ce qu'il y a quelqu'un? [eskeel yah kel-kañ]

   we don't know anybody here nous ne connaissons personne ici [. . . pair-son]

anything: have you got anything for . . . est-ce que vous avez quelque chose pour . . . [. . . kelker-shoz . . .]

   I don't want anything je n'ai besoin de rien [. . . ree-yañ]

aperitif un apéritif

apology des excuses [ex-kooz]

   please accept my apologies je vous prie de m'excuser [jer voo pree der mexkoo-zay]

appellation contrôlée *quality label: a guarantee that a wine comes from one particular area*

appendicitis l'appendicite [ahpān-dee-seet]
appetite: I've lost my appetite j'ai perdu l'appétit
   [. . . ahpay-tee]
apple une pomme
application form un formulaire d'inscription
   [formoo-lair dānskrips-yōn]
appointment un rendez-vous
   can we make an appointment? est-ce que nous
   pouvons prendre rendez-vous? [esker noo poovōn
   prōndr rōnday-voo]
appuyer push
apricot un abricot [ahbree-koh]
April: in April en avril [ān nah-vreel]
aqualung un scaphandre autonome [skah-
   fōndr ohtoh-nohm]
area la région [rayj-yōn]
   in the area dans les environs [. . . ōnvee-rōn]
arm le bras [brah]
around *see* about
arrange: will you arrange it? est-ce que vous pouvez
   vous en occuper? [esker voo poovay voo
   zānn-ohkoo-pay]
   it's all arranged tout est réglé
arrest arrêter [ahray-tay]
arrêt stop
arrival l'arrivée
arrive arriver [ahree-vay]
   we only arrived yesterday nous ne sommes arrivés
   qu'hier
art l'art [ahr]
art gallery un musée [moo-zay]
arthritis: he has arthritis il a de l'arthrite [. . . der
   lar-treet]
artificial artificiel [ahrtee-fees-yel]
artist un artiste [ahr-teest]
as: as big/quickly as possible aussi [ohsee]
   grand/rapidement que possible
   as much/many as you can autant [oh-tōn] que vous
   pouvez
   do as I do faites comme moi [fait kom mwah]
   as you like comme vous voulez [kom voo voolay]
ascenseur lift
ashore à terre [ah tair]

ashtray un cendrier [sōndree-yay]
ask demander [dermōn-day]
  I didn't ask for that ce n'est pas ce que j'ai demandé [ser nay pah ser ker jay . . .]
  could you ask him to . . . est-ce que vous pouvez lui demander de . . . [esker voo poovay . . .]
asleep: he's (still) asleep il dort [dor] (encore)
asparagus des asperges [ass-pairj]
aspirin une aspirine [aspee-reen]
assistant (shop) un vendeur (une vendeuse) [vōn-derr, vōnderz]
asthma: she has asthma elle a de l'asthme [. . . der lassm]
at: at the cafe au [oh] café
  at my hotel à mon hôtel [ah . . .]
  at one o'clock à une heure
atmosphere l'atmosphère [atmoss-fair]
attractive: I think you are very attractive (to woman) je vous trouve très jolie [. . . joh-lee]
  it's an attractive offer c'est une offre avantageuse [. . . ahvōn-tah-jerz]
aubergine une aubergine [ohbair-jeen]
August: in August en août [ōnn-oot]
aunt: my aunt ma tante [tōnt]
Australia l'Australie [ostrah-lee]
  Australian australien [ohstrahl-yān]
authorities les autorités [ohtoh-ree-tay]
automatic automatique
autumn: in the autumn en automne [ōnn-ohton]
away: is it far away from here? est-ce que c'est loin d'ici? [esker-say lwān dee-see]
  go away! allez-vous en! [ahlay voo zōn]
awful affreux [ah-frer]
axle l'essieu [ayss-yer]
baby un bébé
  we'd like a baby-sitter nous cherchons quelqu'un pour garder les enfants [noo shair-shōn kel-kān poor gahr-day layz ōn-fōn]
back (part of body) le dos [doh]
  I've got a bad back je souffre des reins [jer soofr day rān]
  I'll be back soon je reviens dans un moment [jer rerv-yān . . .]

can I have my money back est-ce que vous pouvez
me rendre mon argent?
[esker voo poovay mer rōndr . . .]
come back! revenez! [rerver-nay]
is he back? est-ce qu'il est de retour? [. . . der rer-toor]
I go back tomorrow je rentre demain [jer rōntr
der-mān]
at the back derrière [dair-yair]
bacon le bacon
bacon and eggs du bacon avec des oeufs sur le plat
[. . . ahvek day zer soor ler plah]
bad mauvais [moh-vay]
not bad pas mal [pah mal]
too bad! tant pis! [tōn pee]
bag un sac
(handbag) un sac à main [sak ah mān]
baggage les bagages [bah-gahj]
baignade interdite no bathing
baker's une boulangerie [boolōnj-ree]
balcony balcon [bal-kōn]
ball *(football etc)* un ballon [bah-lōn]
(tennis, golf) une balle [bahl]
ball-point pen un stylo à bille [steeloh ah bee]
banana une banane [bah-nan]
band *(musical)* un orchestre [or-kestr]
bandage: could you change the bandage? est-ce que
vous pouvez changer le bandage? [esker voo poovay
shōnjay ler bōn-dahj]
bank *(establishment)* une banque [bōnk]
(of river) la rive [reev]
» *TRAVEL TIP: opening hours 9-12 and 2-4; closed Sat
(large towns) or Mon; early closing (noon) before a bank
holiday and if bank holiday falls on Thurs may be
closed on Fri as well; transactions carried out at one
desk and money collected at another: 'la caisse'*
bank holiday un jour férié [joor fair-yay]
see **public holidays**
bar un bar
a bar of chocolate une tablette de chocolat [tah-blet
der shohkoh-lah]
barber's le coiffeur [kwah-ferr]
bargain: it's a real bargain c'est une bonne affaire
[sayt oon bon ah-fair]

barmaid la serveuse [sair-verz]
barman le barman [bahr-man]
basket un panier [pan-yay]
bath un bain [bān]; *(tub)* une baignoire [bay-nwahr]
  can I have a bath? est-ce que je peux prendre un
  bain? [esker jer per prōndr in bān]
  bath towel une serviette de bain [sairv-yet . . .]
bathing costume un maillot de bain [may-yoh . . .]
bathroom la salle de bain [sahl der bān]
  we want a room with private bathroom
  nous voulons une chambre avec salle de bain [noo
  voo-lōn oon shōnbr . . .]
battery une pile [peel]
  (in car) la batterie [bat-ree]
be être [aitr]
  I am je suis [jer swee]
  you are vous êtes [voo zait]
  he/she is il/elle est [eelay, ellay]
  it's c'est [say]
  we are nous sommes [noo som]
  they are ils/elles sont [eel sōn]
  he's been ill il a été malade [eel ah ay-tay . . .]
  don't be late ne soyez pas en retard [ner swah-yay
  pah zan rer-tar]
  I am cold/hungry j'ai froid/faim [jay frwah, fān]
beach une plage [plahj]
  on the beach à la plage
  » *TRAVEL TIP: topless bathing on most beaches; pay*
  attention to safety warnings: red flag – no swimming;
  orange flag – unsafe, but lifeguard in attendance; green
  flag – swimming safe
beans des haricots [ahree-koh]
  French beans des haricots verts [. . . vair]
  baked beans *not available as such*
beautiful beau (belle) [boh, bel]
  that was a beautiful meal ce repas était délicieux
  [ser rerpah aytay daylees-yer]
because parce que [pahrser-ker]
  because of the weather à cause du temps
  [ah kohz . . .]
bed un lit [lee]
  I am going to bed at 10 je vais me coucher à dix
  heures [jer vay mer kooshay ah . . .]

you haven't made/changed my bed vous n'avez pas fait mon lit/changé les draps [voo nahvay pah fay mōn lee, shōn-jay lay drah]

bed and breakfast *(terms)* la chambre et le petit déjeuner [lah shōnbr ay ler pertee dayjer-nay]

» *TRAVEL TIP: used to be non-existent as such in France, where there are so many inexpensive hotels; ask the local 'syndicat d'initiative' about the possibility of 'chambres chez l'habitant'*

bedroom une chambre [shōnbr]

bee une abeille [ah-bay]

beef du boeuf [berf]

beer de la bière [bee-yair]

draught beer bière pression [. . . prays-yōn]

» *TRAVEL TIP: for the equivalent of a half-pint of draught lager ask for 'un demi pression'; the standard measure is 330 cl (½ pint = 270 cl); if you simply ask for 'une bière' you may be served bottled beer (more expensive)*

before avant [ah-vōn]

before I leave avant de partir

I haven't been here before c'est la première fois que je viens ici [say lah prerm-yair fwah ker jerv-yān ee-see]

begin commencer [kohmōn-say]

beginner: I'm a beginner je débute [jer day-boot]

behind derrière [dair-yair]

Belgian belge [belj]

Belgium la Belgique [bel-jeek]

believe croire [krwahr]

I don't believe you je ne vous crois [krwah] pas

bell une cloche [klosh]

(at door) la sonnette [soh-net]

belong: that belongs to me c'est à moi [sayt ah mwah]

who does this belong to? à qui est ceci? [ah kee]

below au-dessous (de . . .) [oh der-soo]

belt une ceinture [sān-toor]

bend *(in road)* un virage [vee-rahj]

berries des baies [bay]

berth *(on ship)* une couchette [koo-shet]

beside à côté de [ah koh-tay der]

best: the best . . . le meilleur . . . [may-yerr]

it's the best holiday I've ever had ce sont les meilleures vacances de ma vie

better meilleur [may-yerr]
   haven't you got anything better? est-ce que vous n'avez rien de mieux? [. . . ree-yan der myer]
   are you feeling better? est-ce que vous vous sentez mieux? [esker voo voo sontay myer]
   I'm feeling a lot better je me sens beaucoup mieux
between entre [ontr]
beyond plus loin que [ploo lwan ker]
bicycle une bicyclette [bee-see . . .]
bière (à la) pression draught beer
big grand [gron]
   a big one un grand
   have you got a bigger one? est-ce que vous en avez un plus grand? [esker voo zonn ahvay an ploo gron]
bikini un bikini
bill l'addition [ahdees-yon]
   could I have the bill, please? vous me donnez l'addition, s'il vous plaît [voom doh-nay . . .]
billets tickets
bin *(dustbin)* une poubelle [poo-bel]
bindings *(ski)* les fixations [feexahs-yon]
bird un oiseau [wah-zoh]
birthday: it's my birthday c'est mon anniversaire [ahnee-vair-sair]
   happy birthday! joyeux anniversaire! [jwah-yerz . . .]
bit: a bit of that cake un morceau [mor-soh] de ce gâteau
   just a little bit un petit morceau
   that's a bit too expensive/far c'est un peu trop cher/loin [an-per troh . . .]
bite: insect bites les piqûres d'insectes [pee-koor dan-sekt]
   I've been bitten *(insects)* j'ai été piqué [jay ay-tay pee-kay]
   I've been bitten by a dog j'ai été mordu par un chien [jay aytay mordoo par an shee-yan]
bitter amer [ah-mair]
black noir [nwahr]
   he's had a blackout il a eu une syncope [san-kop]
blanket une couverture [koovair-toor]
bleach de l'eau de javel [ohd jah-vel]
bleed saigner [sayn-yay]

he's bleeding il saigne [sayn]
bless you! *(after sneeze)* à vos souhaits! [ah voh sway]
blind aveugle [ah-vergl]
   blind spot l'angle mort [lōngl-mor]
blister une ampoule [ōnpool]
blocked *(pipe etc)* bouché [boo-shay]
   (road etc) barré [bah-ray]
blonde une blonde [blōnd]
blood le sang [sōn]
   blood test une prise de sang [preez der sōn]
   his blood group is . . . son groupe sanguin est . . .
   [sōn groop sōn-ghān ay]
   I've got high blood pressure j'ai de la tension [jayd
   lah tōns-yōn]
   he needs a blood transfusion il faut lui faire une
   transfusion [trōns-fooz-yōn] de sang
blouse un chemisier [shermeez-yay]
blue bleu [bler]
board: full board la pension complète [pōns-yōn
   kōn-plet]
   half board la demi-pension
   boarding pass la carte d'embarquement
   [. . . dōnbar-ker-mōn]
boat un bateau [bah-toh]
body le corps [kor]
bodywork la carrosserie [kahross-ree]
boil *(on skin)* un furoncle [foo-rōnkl]
   (verb) bouillir [boo-yeer]
   it's boiling ça bout [sah boo]
   do we have to boil the water? est-ce qu'il faut faire
   bouillir l'eau? [eskeel foh fair . . .]
   boiled egg un oeuf à la coque [ān erf ah lah kok]
bone un os [oss]
   (in fish) une arête [ah-ret]
bonnet *(of car)* le capot [kah-poh]
book *(noun)* un livre [leevr]
   (verb) réserver [rayzair-vay]
   book of stamps carnet de timbres [karnay der tānbr]
   can I book a seat? est-ce que je peux réserver une
   place?
   we have booked a table for 2 nous avons réservé
   une table pour deux [noo zahvōn rayzair-vay oon tahbl
   poor der]

booking office le guichet [ghee-shay]
bookshop une librairie [leebray-ree]
boot *(of car)* le coffre [kofr]
  (shoe) une chaussure [shoh-soor]
booze: I had too much booze last night j'ai trop bu
  hier soir [jay troh boo . . .]
border la frontière [front-yair]
bored: I'm bored je m'ennuie [jer mon-nwee]
boring ennuyeux [on-nwee-yer]
born: I was born in je suis né en [jer swee nay on]
borrow: can I borrow . . .? est-ce que je peux
  emprunter . . .? [esker jer per onpran-tay]
boss le chef [shef]
both les deux [lay der]
  I'll take both of them je prends les deux
bottle une bouteille [boo-tey]
  (for baby) un biberon [beeb-ron]
  bottle-opener un ouvre-bouteille [oovr-boo-tey]
bottom: at the bottom of the hill au pied de la colline
  [oh pyay der lah koh-leen]
bowels les intestins [antes-tan]
bowl une coupe [koop]
 bowls *(game)* les boules [bool]
box une boîte [bwaht]; *(in theatre)* une loge [lohj]
boy un garçon [gar-son]
boyfriend: my boyfriend mon ami [ah-mee]
bra un soutien-gorge [soot-yan-gorj]
bracelet un bracelet [brahs-lay]
braces les bretelles [brer-tel]
brake *(verb)* freiner [fray-nay]
  can you check the brakes? est-ce que vous pouvez
  vérifier les freins? [. . . lay-fran]
  I had to brake suddenly j'ai dû freiner tout à coup
  [jay doo fray-nay too tah koo]
  he didn't brake il n'a pas freiné
brandy le cognac [kohn-yak]
bread du pain [pan]
  a loaf of bread un pain
  sliced bread du pain en tranches [tronsh]
  wholemeal bread du pain entier [ont-yay]
  could we have some bread and butter?
  est-ce que vous pouvez nous apporter du pain avec du
  beurre? [. . . doo pan ahvek doo berr]

» *TRAVEL TIP: French bread is an entirely new
experience after the sliced loaf; ask for 'une baguette'*
[oon bah-ghet] *(best eaten the same day)*

break casser [kah-say]
  I think I've broken my leg/arm je crois que je me
suis cassé la jambe/le bras [. . . jer mer swee kahsay lah
jonb, ler brah]
  the car broke down la voiture est tombée en panne
[lah vwahtoor ay tōn-bay ōn pan]
breakable fragile [frah-jeel]
breakdown *(of car)* une panne [pan]
  (nervous) une dépression nerveuse [daypress-yōn
nair-verz]
breakfast le petit déjeuner [pertee dayjer-nay]
  English breakfast un petit déjeuner à l'anglaise
[. . . ah lōnglayz]
» *TRAVEL TIP: the French don't have a cooked breakfast;
usually coffee with bread and butter or croissants; if you
insist on an English breakfast, be prepared to pay more*
breast le sein [sān]
breath: he's getting very short of breath il a de la
peine à respirer [eelah der lah pen ah respee-ray]
  breathe [respee-ray]
  I can't breathe j'ai de la peine à respirer
bridge un pont [pōn]
  (game) le bridge
briefcase une serviette [sairv-yet]
brighten up: will it brighten up later? est-ce que ça
va s'éclaircir plus tard? [. . . sayklair-seer . . .]
brilliant brillant [bree-yōn]
bring apporter [ahpor-tay]
  bring the case to my hotel apportez la valise à mon
hôtel
Britain la Grande-Bretagne [grōnd-brer-tan]
  British britannique [breetah-neek]
Brittany la Bretagne [brer-tan]
brochure un prospectus [prospek-toos]
  have you got any brochures about . . .?
est-ce que vous avez des prospectus sur . . .?
broken: it's broken c'est cassé [say kah-say]
  my room/car has been broken into quelqu'un s'est
introduit [say tān-troh-dwee] dans ma
chambre/voiture

brooch une broche [brosh]
brother: my brother mon frère [frair]
brown brun (brune) [brãn, broon]
  brown paper du papier d'emballage
  [pahp-yay dōnbah-lahj]
browse: can I just browse around? est-ce que je peux
  regarder? [esker jer per rergahr-day]
bruise une contusion [kōntooz-yōn]
brunette une brune [broon]
brush une brosse [bross]
  (painter's) un pinceau [pãn-soh]
Brussels sprouts des choux de Bruxelles [shoo der
  broo-sel]
bucket un seau [soh]
buffet un buffet [boo-fay]
  buffet car un wagon restaurant [vah-gōn . . .]
building un bâtiment [bahtee-mōn]
  (residential) un immeuble [ee-merbl]
bulb une ampoule [ōn-pool]
  the bulb's gone l'ampoule a sauté
  [lōn-pool ah sohtay]
  a 100 watt bulb une ampoule de cent watts
  [. . . der sōn wat]
bump: he's had a bump on the head il s'est tapé la
  tête [eel say tah-pay lah tet]
bumper le pare-chocs [par-shock]
bunch of flowers un bouquet [boo-kay]
bunk une couchette [koo-shet]
  bunk beds des lits superposés [lee soopair-poh-zay]
buoy une bouée [boo-ay]
burglar un cambrioleur [kōnbree-oh-lerr]
  our flat's been burgled on a cambriolé
  [kōnbree-oh-lay] notre appartement
burn: can you give me something for burns? est-ce
  que vous avez quelque chose pour les brûlures? [esker
  voo zah-vay kelker-shohz poor lay broo-loor]
  this meat is burnt cette viande est brûlée [broo-lay]
  my arms are burnt j'ai un coup de soleil aux bras
  [jay ãn koo der soh-lay . . .]
bus l'autobus [otoh-booss]
  by bus en autobus
  bus stop l'arrêt d'autobus [ahray . . .]
  bus station la gare routière [gahr root-yair]

could you tell me when we get there? est-ce que vous pouvez m'avertir quand on y arrive? [esker voo poovay mahvair-teer kān tōn nee ah-reev]

» *TRAVEL TIP: pay-as-you-enter in most cities; you can buy a 'carnet de tickets' (book of tickets) from a newsagent; you must punch your ticket when boarding the bus and use 2 tickets if you are travelling further than two fare stages as shown on the bus route chart; runabout 'billets touristiques' available for bus and underground services*

business les affaires [ah-fair]
  (firm) une entreprise [ōntrer-preez]
  I'm here on business je suis ici pour affaires [jer swee zeesee . . .]
  business trip un voyage [voh-yahj] d'affaires
  it's none of your business cela ne vous regarde pas [ser-lah ner voo rer-gard pah]

bust la poitrine [pwah-treen]

» *TRAVEL TIP: bust measurements*

UK	32	34	36	38	40
France	80	87	91	97	102

busy occupé [ohkoo-pay]
  are you busy? est-ce que vous êtes occupé?

but mais [may]

butcher's une boucherie [boosh-ree]

butter du beurre [berr]

button un bouton [boo-tōn]

buy acheter [ash-tay]
  I'll buy it je l'achète [jer lah-shet]

by: I'm here by myself je suis venu seul [jer swee vernoo serl]
  are you here by yourself? est-ce que vous êtes venu seul?
  can you do it by tomorrow? est-ce que vous pouvez le faire d'ici à demain? [. . . dee-see ah der-mān]
  by train/car/plane en [ōn] train/voiture/avion
  by the church près de l'église [pray der . . .]
  who's it made by? c'est fabriqué par qui?

cabaret un spectacle [spek-tahkl] de variétés

cabbage un chou [shoo]

cabin *(on ship)* une cabine [kah-been]

cable un câble [kahbl]

cable car un téléphérique [taylay-fay-reek]

cafe un restaurant-snack
 » *TRAVEL TIP: the equivalent of a transport cafe is called 'relais routier', where good and relatively inexpensive meals can be had*
café *the usual place for a drink; waiter service, children usually welcome; drinks cheaper at the bar; snacks or set lunch usually available; you can telephone from a 'café' and there is often a special counter where stamps and tobacco are sold: look for a red diamond shaped 'TABAC' sign outside; you generally pay for your drinks on leaving*
cake un gâteau [gah-toh]
 (small) un petit gâteau
caisse *cash desk*
calculator un calculateur [kalkoo-lah-terr]
call: will you call the manager est-ce que vous pouvez appeler le gérant [. . . ap-lay ler jay-rōn]
 what is this called? comment ça s'appelle? [komōn sah sah-pel]
 call box une cabine téléphonique [kah-been taylay-foh-neek]
 see also **telephone**
calm calme
 calm down! calmez-vous! [kalmay-voo]
camera un appareil-photo [appah-rey . . .]
camp: where can we camp? où est-ce qu'on peut camper? [weskōn per kōn-pay]
 can we camp here? est-ce qu'on peut camper ici?
 we are on a camping holiday nous faisons [fer-zōn] du camping
 campsite un terrain [tay-rān] de camping
 » *TRAVEL TIP: enquire at the local 'syndicat d'initiative' (tourist office) about location, rates and facilities; you may have to leave your passport at the campsite reception desk; International Camping Carnet not essential, but it may help or entitle you to a discount*
can¹: a can of beer une bière en boîte
 (NB: *bottled beer is the rule*)
 can-opener un ouvre-boîte [oovr-bwaht]
can²: can I have . . .? est-ce que je peux avoir . . .? [esker jer per ah-vwahr]
 can you show me . . .? est-ce que vous pouvez me montrer . . .?

I can't swim je ne sais pas nager [jer ner say pah]
   he can't . . . il ne peut pas . . .
   we can't . . . nous ne pouvons [poo-vōn] pas . . .
Canada le Canada [kahnah-dah]
   Canadian canadien [kahnahd-yān]
cancel: I want to cancel my booking je veux annuler
   ma réservation [jer ver ahnoo-lay mah
   rayzair-vahs-yōn]
   can we cancel dinner for tonight? est-ce
   que nous pouvons décommander le dîner ce soir?
   [. . . day-koh-mōn day ler dee-nay . . .]
candle une bougie [boo-jee]
capsize chavirer [shahvee-ray]
car une voiture [vwah-toor]
   car keys les clés de la voiture [klay . . .]
   by car en voiture
   car park un parking
carafe une carafe [kah-raf]
caravan une caravane [kahrah-van]
   caravan site un camping pour caravanes
carburettor le carburateur [karboo-rah-terr]
card une carte
   do you play cards? est-ce que vous jouez aux cartes?
   [esker voo jway oh kart]
care: will you take care of this for me? est-ce que
   vous pouvez vous en occuper?
   [. . . voo-zōn noh-koo-pay]
   goodbye, take care au revoir [oh rer-vwahr]
careful: be careful soyez prudent [swah-yay-
   proo-dōn]
car-ferry un ferry
carnation un oeillet [er-yay]
carpet un tapis [tah-pee]
carrots des carottes [kah-rot]
carry porter [por-tay]
   will you carry this for me? est-ce que vous pouvez
   me porter ça? [esker voo poovay mer pohr-tay sah]
carry-cot un porte-bébé [pohrt-baybay]
cartridge une cartouche [kahr-toosh]
carving une sculpture [skoolp-toor]
case *(suitcase)* une valise [vah-leez]
cash: I haven't any cash je n'ai pas d'argent liquide
   [jer nay pah dahr-jōn-lee-keed]

will you cash a cheque for me? est-ce que vous
pouvez me payer [pay-yay] un chèque?
I'll pay cash je paye comptant [jer pay kōn-tōn]
cash desk la caisse [kes]
casino un casino [kahzee-no]
casse-croûte snack(s)
cassette une cassette [kah-set]
castle un château [shah-toh]
» *TRAVEL TIP: most castles and museums are closed on
Tuesdays in France*
cat un chat [shah]
catch attraper [ahtrah-pay]
where do we catch the bus? où est-ce qu'on prend
l'autobus? [weskōn-prōn-lohtoh-boos]
he's caught a bug il a attrapé un virus [vee-roos]
cathedral la cathédrale [kahtay-drahl]
catholic catholique [kahtoh-leek]
cauliflower un chou-fleur [shoo-flerr]
cave une grotte [grot]
ceiling le plafond [plah-fōn]
celery du céleri en branche [sail-ree ōn brōnsh]
» *TRAVEL TIP: if you see 'céleri' on the menu, it will
probably be 'celeriac'; 'céleri rémoulade' is a celeriac
salad eaten as a first course*
centigrade centigrade [sōntee-grad]
» *TRAVEL TIP: to convert C to F*

$$\frac{C}{5} \times 9 + 32 = F$$

*centigrade   −5   0   10   15   21   30   36,9
Fahrenheit   23   32   50   59   70   86   98.4*
centimetre un centimètre [sōntee-maitr]
» *TRAVEL TIP: 1 cm = 0.39 inches*
central central [sōn-trahl]
with central heating avec le chauffage [shoh-fahj]
central
centre le centre [sōntr]
centre-ville city centre, town centre
cereal: *name the one you want:*'les Corn Flakes' *is the
best known*
certain certain (certaine) [sair-tān, –ten]
are you certain? est-ce que vous en êtes sûr? [esker
voo zōn nait soor]
certificate un certificat [sairtee-fee-kah]

chain une chaîne [shairn]
chair une chaise [shairz]
   (easy chair) un fauteuil [foh-ter]
chairlift un télésiège [taylays-yej]
chambermaid la femme de chambre [fam der shōnbr]
chambres rooms to let
champagne du champagne [shōn-pan]
change changer [shōn-jay]
   where can I change some money? où est-ce que je
   peux changer de l'argent? [wesker jer per shōn-jay der
   lahr-jōn]
   could you change this into francs? est-ce que vous
   pouvez me changer ça en francs?
   [. . . mer shōn-jay sah ōn frōn]
   I haven't any change je n'ai pas de monnaie [jer nay
   pah der moh-nay]
   do you have change for 10 francs? est-ce que vous
   avez la monnaie de dix francs?
   small change de la petite monnaie
   do we have to change trains? est-ce qu'il faut
   changer? [eskeel foh . . .]
   where can I get changed? où est-ce que je peux me
   changer?
 » *TRAVEL TIP: changing money: remember you can buy
   up to £50 worth of foreign currency with your own
   cheques and a valid banker's card with Eurocheque
   symbol; exchange rate most favourable in a bank*
Channel: the Channel la Manche [monsh]
Channel Islands les îles anglo-normandes [eel ōn-gloh
nor-mōnd]
chantier roadworks
charge: what will you charge? combien est-ce que ça
   va coûter? [kōnb-yān esker sah vah koo-tay]
   who's in charge? qui est le responsable
   [respōnsahbl] ici?
chart *(map)* une carte maritime [. . . mahree-teem]
chaud hot
chaussée verglacée icy road surface
cheap bon marché [bōn mahr-shay]
   is there anything cheaper? est-ce qu'il y a quelque
   chose de meilleur marché? [. . . may-yer mahr-shay]
cheat: I've been cheated je me suis fait avoir [jer mer
swee fay ah-vwahr]

....

check: will you check? est-ce que vous pouvez vérifier
[. . . vayreef-yay]
   I'm sure, I've checked j'en suis sûr, j'ai vérifié
   we checked in/we checked out at 10 nous sommes
   arrivés/partis à dix heures
cheek *(part of face)* la joue [joo]
cheers! *(toast)* santé! [sōn-tay]
cheerio *(bye)* au revoir! [oh rer-vwahr]
cheese du fromage [froh-mahj]
   mild/strong cheese du fromage doux/fort
   [. . . doo, for]
» *TRAVEL TIP: cheese is always served before the sweet
course; don't ask for biscuits, as bread is usually eaten
with cheese; there is a bewildering variety of cheeses:
ask to sample before buying*
chef le chef cuisinier [. . . kweezeen-yay]
chemist's une pharmacie [farmah-see]
» *TRAVEL TIP: often with green cross sign; most will
make up a prescription; address of chemist on all-night
or Sunday duty ('pharmacie de garde') in local paper or
on door of every 'pharmacie'*
cheque un chèque [shek]
   cheque book le carnet de chèques
   cheque card la carte d'identité bancaire [kart
   deedōn-tee-tay bōn-kair]
» *TRAVEL TIP: you won't be able to pay in a shop with
your own cheques, but remember you can buy foreign
currency with your cheques and your Eurocard*
chess les échecs [ay-sheck]
chest la poitrine [pwah-treen]
» *TRAVEL TIP: chest measurements ('tour de poitrine')*

UK	34	36	38	40	42	44	46
France	87	91	97	102	107	112	117

cherries des cerises [ser-reez]
chewing gum du chewing-gum [shween-gom]
chicken du poulet [poo-lay]
chickenpox la varicelle [vahree-sel]
child un enfant [ōn-fōn]
   my children mes enfants
   children's portions des portions [pors-yōn] pour
   enfants
» *TRAVEL TIP: children are generally welcome in
restaurants and cafés*

chin le menton [mon-ton]
china la porcelaine [por-ser-lain]
chips des frites [freet]
  (at casino) des plaques [plak]
chocolate du chocolat [shohkoh-lah]
  a box of chocolates une boîte [bwaht] de chocolats
  hot chocolate un chocolat chaud [. . . shoh]
  milk chocolate du chocolat au lait [. . . oh-lay]
  plain chocolate du chocolat à croquer [. . . ah
  kroh-kay]
choke *(car)* le starter [star-tair]
chop: a pork chop une côtelette de porc [koht-let der
  por]
Christian name le prénom [pray-non]
Christmas: at Christmas à Noël [noh-el]
  on Christmas Eve la veille [vey] de Noël
  Happy Christmas joyeux [jwah-yer] Noël
  » *TRAVEL TIP: Christmas Eve is usually an occasion for*
  a big meal with the family or friends, 'le réveillon'
  [rayvay-yon]
church une église [ay-gleez]
  » *TRAVEL TIP: France being largely a catholic country*
  there are few protestant churches; ask for 'le temple'
  [tonpl]; *in big cities, you may find 'une église anglicane'*
  [onglee-kan] *(C. of E.)*
chutes de pierres *falling rocks*
cider du cidre [seedr]
cigar un cigare [see-gar]
cigarette une cigarette [seegah-ret]
  would you like a cigarette? est-ce que je peux vous
  offrir une cigarette?
  [esker jer per voo zoh-freer . . .]
  tipped filtre
  plain sans filtre [son feeltr]
cine-camera une caméra [kahmay-rah]
cinema un cinéma [seenay-mah]
  » *TRAVEL TIP: tip the usherette; no smoking*
circle un cercle [sairkl]
  (at cinema) le balcon [bal-kon]
circuit touristique *scenic route*
city une ville [veel]
  city centre le centre-ville
  [sontrer-veel]

claim *(insurance)* une demande d'indemnité [der-mãnd dãndem-nee-tay]

claret du bordeaux rouge [bor-doh rooj]

clarify clarifier [klahreef-yay]

class: 1st class, 2nd class première classe, deuxième classe [prerm-yair klas, derz-yem . . .]

clean *(adjective)* propre [prohpr]
   can I have some clean sheets? est-ce que je peux avoir des draps [drah] propres?
   my room hasn't been cleaned today on n'a pas nettoyé ma chambre aujourd'hui
   it's not clean ce n'est pas propre

cleansing cream crème démaquillante [daymah-kee-yõnt]

clear: I'm not clear about it je n'ai pas bien compris
   is the road clear? est-ce que la route est dégagée? [. . . daygah-jay]

clever intelligent (intelligente) [ãntay-lee-jon]

climate le climat [klee-mah]

climb: we're going to climb . . . nous allons escalader . . . [eskah-lah-day]
   climber un alpiniste [alpee-neest]
   climbing boots des chaussures d'escalade [shoh-soor deskah-lad]

» *TRAVEL TIP: beware of rapidly changing weather conditions; let somebody know where you plan to go; ask the local C.A.F. (Club Alpin Français) for information; the C.A.F. have an excellent network of huts ('refuges' and 'chalets-refuges')*

cloakroom le vestiaire [vest-yair]
   (WC) les toilettes [twah-let]

clock une horloge [or-lohj]

close¹: it's close today il fait lourd aujourd'hui [eel fay loor . . .]
   is it close? est-ce que c'est près d'ici? [esker say pray dee-see]

close² *(verb)* fermer [fair-may]
   closed fermé
   when do you close? quand est-ce que vous fermez?

cloth le tissu [tee-soo]
   (for wiping) un chiffon [shee-fõn]

clothes les vêtements [vet-mõn]

cloud un nuage [noo-ahj]

clutch l'embrayage [ōnbray-yahj]
  the clutch is slipping l'embrayage patine
  [. . . pah-teen]
coach un autocar [υtoh-kar]
  coach tour une excursion en autocar
  [exkoors-yōn . . .]
coast la côte [koht]
  coastguard le garde-côte [gahrd-koht]
coat un manteau [mōn-toh]
cockroach un cafard [kah-far]
coffee un café [kah-fay]
  white coffee café au lait [. . . oh lay]
  black coffee café noir [. . . nwahr]
» *TRAVEL TIP: if you want a small black coffee, ask for 'un*
  café petite tasse', for a large black coffee: 'un café grande
  tasse'; white coffee as you know it is not served; 'café au
  lait' is hot milk with hot black coffee; 'café crème' is
  black coffee with a drop of milk or cream
coin une pièce de monnaie [pee-yes der moh-nay]
  the coin is stuck la pièce est
  coincée [. . . kwān-say]
coke *(drink)* un coca-cola
cold froid [frwah]
  I'm cold j'ai froid
  I've got a cold j'ai un rhume [jay ān room]
collapse: **he's collapsed** il s'est effondré [ayfōn-dray]
collar le col [kol]
» *TRAVEL TIP: continental sizes*

Continental	36	37	38	39		41	42	43
UK (old)	14	14½	15	15½	16	16½	17	

colleague un(une) collègue [koh-leg]
collect: **I want to collect . . .** je viens chercher . . .
  [. . . shair-shay]
collision une collision [kohleez-yōn]
colour la couleur [koo-lerr]
  have you any other colours? est-ce que vous avez
  d'autres couleurs?
comb un peigne [pen]
come venir [ver-neer]
  I come/we come from London je viens/nous venons
  de Londres [jer vee-yān, noo ver-nōn . . .]
  when is he coming? quand est-ce qu'il vient?
  [kōntesk-eel vee-yān]

we came here yesterday nous sommes arrivés [noo somz ahree-vay] ici hier
come with me venez [ver-nay] avec moi
has he come back yet? est-ce qu'il est rentré?
come on! allons!
comfortable: it's not very comfortable ce n'est pas très confortable [. . . kōnfor-tahbl]
Common Market le Marché commun [marshay koh-mān]
communication cord le signal d'alarme [seen-yal dah larm]
company une société [sohssay-tay]
    I like your company j'aime votre compagnie [jaym vohtr kōnpah-nee]
compartment *(train)* un compartiment [kōnpar-tee-mōn]
compass une boussole [boo-sohl]
compensation: I demand compensation je veux être dédommagé [. . . daydoh-mah-jay]
complain: I want to complain about . . . je désire réclamer au sujet de . . . [rayklah-may oh soo-jay der]
    have you got a complaints book? est-ce que vous avez un registre [rer-jeestr] des réclamations?
complet *no vacancies*
completely complètement [kōnplet-mōn]
complicated compliqué [kōnplee-kay]
compliment: my compliments to the chef mes compliments [kōnplee-mōn] au chef
composter: prière de composter votre billet *please punch your ticket here*
compulsory: is it compulsory? est-ce que c'est obligatoire? [. . . ohblee-gah-twahr]
concern: I'm concerned about . . . je suis inquiet au sujet de . . . [jer swee ānk-yay oh soo-jay der]
concert un concert
concierge *caretaker*
concussion une commotion cérébrale [kohmohs-yōn sayray-brahl]
condition: it's not in very good condition ce n'est pas en très bon état [ser nay pah ōn tray bohn ay-tah]
    what are your conditions? quelles sont vos conditions? [kel sōn voh kōn-dees-yōn]
confection *ready-to-wear*

conference une conférence [kōnfay-rōns]
confirm confirmer [kōnfeer-may]
congés holiday
congratulations félicitations [faylee-see-tahs-yōn]
conjunctivitis une conjonctivite [kōnjōnk-tee-veet]
connection (train etc) la correspondance
   [kohres-pōn-dōns]
connoisseur un connaisseur [kohnay-ser]
conscious conscient [kōns-yān]
consciousness: he's lost consciousness il a perdu
   connaissance [... kohnay-sāns]
consigne left luggage
constipation la constipation [kōnstee-pah-syōn]
consul le consul [kōn-sool]
consulate le consulat [kōnsoo-lah]
contact: how can I contact ...? comment est-ce que
   je peux contacter ...? [kohmōn esker jer per
   kōntak-tay]
   contact lenses les verres [vair] de contact
contraceptive un contraceptif [kōntrah sep-teef]
convenient pratique [prah-teek]
cook cuire [kweer]
   it's not cooked ce n'est pas cuit [ser nay pah kwee]
   you are a good cook vous faites une excellente
   cuisine [voo fair oon exay-lōnt kwee-zeen]
   are there any cooking facilities? est-ce qu'on peut y
   faire sa cuisine? [eskōn per ee fair ...]
   cooker la cuisinière [kweezee-nyair]
cool frais (fraîche) [fray, fresh]
corkscrew le tire-bouchon [teerboo-shōn]
corn (on foot) un cor au pied [kohrohp-yay]
corner (bend) un virage [vee-rahj]
   can we have a corner table? est-ce qu'on peut avoir
   une table d'angle? [eskōn per ah-vwahr oon tahbl
   dōngl]
cornflakes des cornflakes
correct correct
cosmetics des produits de beauté [prohdwee der
   boh-tay]
cost: what does it cost? combien ça coûte? [kōnb-yān
   sah koot]
cot un lit d'enfant [lee dōn-fōn]
cotton du coton [koh-tōn]

cotton wool du coton hydrophile [. . . eedroh-feel]
couchette une couchette [koo-shet]
cough la toux [too]
  cough drops des bonbons [bōnbōn] pour la toux
  cough mixture un sirop [see-roh] pour la toux
could: could you please . . .? est-ce que vous
  pouvez . . .? [esker voo poo-vay]
  could I have . . .? est-ce que je peux avoir . . .? [esker
  jer per ah-vwahr]
  we couldn't . . . nous n'avons pas pu . . . [noo nah-vōn
  pah poo]
country un pays [payee]
  in the country à la campagne [ah lah kōn-pan]
couple: a couple of . . . quelques . . . [kelk]
courier l'accompagnateur [ahkōn-pahn-yah-terr]
course: first course l'entrée [ōn-tray]
  main course le plat principal [plah prānsee-pal]
  meat course le plat de viande [. . . vee-yōnd]
  of course naturellement [nahtoo-rel-mōn]
court: I'll take you to court je vais vous poursuivre en
  justice [. . . poorsweevr-ōn-joos-tees]
cousin: my cousin mon cousin [koo-zān]
cover *(verb)* couvrir [koo-vreer]
  keep him well covered couvrez-le bien
  cover charge le couvert [koo-vair]
cow une vache [vash]
crab un crabe [krahb]
craft shop une boutique d'artisanat [. . . artee-zah-nah]
crash: there's been a crash il y a eu une collision
  [eelyah oo oon kohleez-yōn]
  crash helmet un casque [kahsk]
crazy: you're crazy vous êtes fou (folle)
cream de la crème [kraym]
creche une crèche [kraysh]
credit card une carte de crédit [. . . kray-dee]
crêperie pancake shop
crisps des chips [cheeps]
cross *(noun)* une croix [krwah]
  (verb) traverser [trahvair-say]
crossroads un carrefour [kar-foor]
crowded: it's crowded il y a beaucoup de monde
  [eelyah bohkoo-der-mōnd]
cruise une croisière [krwahz-yair]

crutch une béquille [bay-kee]
  (*crotch*) l'entre-jambes [ontr-jonb]
cry: don't cry ne pleurez pas [pler-ray ...]
cufflink un bouton de manchette [boo-ton der
  mon-shet]
cup une tasse [tahs]
  a cup of coffee/tea un café/thé [kah-fay, tay]
cupboard une armoire [arm-wahr]
curry un plat au curry [plah oh ker-ree]
curtains les rideaux [ree-doh]
cushion un coussin [koo-san]
Customs la douane [dwahn]
cut couper [koo-pay]
  I've cut myself je me suis coupé [jer mer swee
  koo-pay]
cycle: can we cycle there? est-ce qu'on peut y aller à
  bicyclette? [eskon per ee ah-lay ah beesee-klet]
cyclist un cycliste [see-kleest]
cylinder un cylindre [see-landr]
  cylinder head gasket un joint de culasse [jwan der
  koo-lass]
damage: I'll pay for the damage je rembourserai les
  dégâts [jer ronboor-ser-ray lay day-gah]
  it's damaged c'est abîmé [... ahbee-may]
damp humide [oo-mid]
dames ladies' toilets
dance: is there a dance on? est-ce qu'il y a une soirée
  dansante? [eskeelyah oon swah-ray don-sont]
  would you like to dance? voulez-vous danser?
  [voolay-voo don-say]
dangerous dangereux [donj-rer]
dark (*colour*) foncé [fon-say]
  dark blue bleu foncé [bler ...]
  when does it get dark? quand est-ce que la nuit
  tombe? [kontesker lah nwee-tonb]
darling: my darling (*to man*) mon chéri
  [mon shay-ree]
  (*to lady*) ma chérie [mah ...]
dashboard le tableau de bord [tahbloh der bor]
date (*fruit*) une datte [dat]
  (*time*) la date [dat]
  what's the date today? quelle est la date
  d'aujourd'hui? [kel ay lah dat dohjoor-dwee]

can we make a date? est-ce que nous pouvons fixer un rendez-vous? [esker noo poovōn feexay an rōnday-voo]

it's the 1st of February c'est le premier février [prerm-yay . . .]

on the 2nd of February le deux février *(NB: except for the 1st of the month, use 'deux', 'trois' etc and not 'deuxième' etc)*

in 1983 en dix-neuf cent quatre-vingt trois [deez-ner-sōn kah-trer-vān trwah]

daughter: my daughter ma fille [fee]

day un jour [joor]

  by day de jour

  the day after le lendemain [lōnder-mān]

  the day before la veille [vay]

dazzle: his lights were dazzling me ses phares m'éblouissaient [. . . maybloo-ee-say]

dead mort [mor]

deaf sourd [soor]

deal un marché [mahr-shay]

  it's a deal! d'accord! [dah-kor]

  will you deal with it? est-ce que vous pouvez vous en charger? [esker voo poovay voo zōn shar-jay]

dealer: the BL dealer le concessionnaire British Leyland [kōnsess-yoh-nair . . .]

dear cher [shair]; *see* letter

December: in December en décembre [day-sōnbr]

deck le pont [pōn]

  deckchair une chaise longue [shayz lōng]

declare: I have nothing to declare je n'ai rien à déclarer [jer nay ree-yān nah dayklah-ray]

deep: is it deep? est-ce que c'est profond? [esker say proh-fōn]

défense d'entrer no entry

de-icer le dégivreur [day-jee-vrer]

delay un retard [rer-tahr]

  the flight was delayed le vol a eu du retard [ler vol ah oo doo . . .]

deliberately exprès [ex-pray]

delicate délicat [daylee-kah]

delicatessen une épicerie fine [ay-pees-ree-feen]

delicious délicieux [daylees-yer]

deliver livrer [lee-vray]

delivery *(of goods)* la livraison [leevray-z̄on]
  (of mail) la distribution [deestree-boos-ȳon]
de luxe de luxe [der-looks]
democratic démocratique [daymoh-krah-teek]
demonstration une démonstration [. . .–trahs-ȳon]
  (political etc) une manifestation [. . –tahs-ȳon]
dent une bosse [boss]
  you've dented my car vous avez endommagé ma
  carosserie [. . .ōndoh-mah-jay . . .]
dentist un dentiste [d̄on-teest]
  YOU MAY HEAR . . .
  ouvrez! *open wide,* rincez! *you can rinse now*
dentures un dentier [d̄ont-yay]
deny: I deny it ce n'est pas vrai [ser nay pah vray]
deodorant un déodorant [day-oh-doh-r̄on]
dépannage breakdown recovery service
departure le départ [day-par]
depend: it depends *(on)* ça dépend [day-p̄on] (de)
deposit *(down payment)* un acompte [ah-k̄ont]
  (security) une caution [kohs-ȳon]
  (on bottle etc) la consigne [k̄on-seen]
  do I have to pay a deposit? est-ce qu'il faut verser
  un acompte? [eskeel foh vair-say ān ah-k̄ont]
depressed déprimé [daypree-may]
depth la profondeur [prohf̄on-derr]
desperate: I'm desperate for a drink je meurs de soif
  [jer merr ·er swahf]
dessert un dessert [day-sair]
» *TRAVEL TIP: always served after cheese*
destination la destination [destee-nahs-ȳon]
detergent un détergent [daytair-j̄on]
detour un détour [day-toor]
devalued dévalué [dayvah-loo-ay]
develop: could you develop these? est-ce que vous
  pouvez me développer [dayv-loh-pay] ces films?
diabetic diabétique [dee-yah-bay-teek]
dial le cadran [kah-dr̄on]
  dialling code l'indicatif [āndee-kah-teef]
  dialling tone la tonalité [tohnah-lee-tay]
diamond un diamant [dee-yah-m̄on]
diarrhoea: have you got something for
  diarrhoea? est-ce que vous avez quelque chose pour
  la diarrhée? [. . . kel-ker shohz poor lah dee-yah-ray]

....

diary un agenda [ahj̄on-dah]
dictionary un dictionnaire [deeks-yoh-nair]
didn't *see* not
die mourir [moo-reer]
  he's dying il est mourant [moo-r̄on]
diesel *(fuel)* du gas-oil [gahz-wahl]
diet un régime [ray-jeem]
  I'm on a diet je suis au régime [jer swee . . .]
different différent [deefay-r̄on]
  can I have a different room? est-ce que je peux avoir
  une autre chambre? [esker jer per ah-vwahr oon ohtr
  sh̄onbr]
difficult difficile [deefee-seel]
digestion la digestion [deejest-ȳon]
dinghy *(rubber)* un canot pneumatique
  [kah-noh pnermah-teek]
  (sailing) un dériveur [dayree-verr]
dining car la voiture-restaurant [vwah-toor . . .]
dining room la salle à manger [sahlah-m̄on-jay]
dinner le dîner [dee-nay]
  dinner jacket un smoking
**dipped headlights: I was using dipped
  headlights** je roulais en code [jer roo-lay ̄on kod]
direct: does it go direct? est-ce que c'est direct?
  [. . . dee-rekt]
directory *(telephone)* l'annuaire [ah-nwair] du
  téléphone
dirty sale [sahl]
disabled handicapé [̄ondee-kah-pay]
disappear disparaître [deespah-raitr]
disappointing décevant [days-v̄on]
disco une discothèque [–tek]
discount un rabais [rah-bay]
disgusting dégoûtant [daygoo-t̄on]
dish un plat [plah]
dishonest malhonnête [mahloh-net]
disinfectant un désinfectant [dayz̄an-fek-t̄on]
dispensing chemist une pharmacie [fahrmah-see]
» *TRAVEL TIP: most 'pharmacies' are dispensing
  chemists*
distance la distance [dees-t̄ons]
  in the distance au loin [lw̄an]
distilled water de l'eau distillée [oh deestee-lay]

distress signal un signal de détresse [seen-yal der day-tres]

distributor *(on car)* le delco [del-koh]

district le quartier [kart-yay]

disturb déranger [day-rōn-jay]

   the noise is disturbing us le bruit [brwee] nous dérange

diving board le plongeoir [plōn-jwahr]

divorced: I'm divorced je suis divorcé [jer swee deevohr-say]

do faire [fair]

   how do you do? comment allez-vous? [koh-mōnt ah-lay voo]

   can I do this? est-ce que je peux faire ça? [esker jer per fair sah]

   what are you doing tonight? qu'est-ce que vous faites ce soir? [kesker voo fayt ser swahr]

   how do you do it? comment est-ce que vous faites? [koh-mōnt esker voo fayt]

   what did you do? qu'est-ce que vous avez fait? [kesker vooz ah-vay fay]

   will you do it for me? est-ce que vous pouvez le faire pour moi?

   I've never done it before je n'ai jamais fait ça [. . . jah-may fay sah]

   I was doing 60 kph je roulais à soixante [jer roo-lay ah swah-sōnt]

doctor un docteur [dok-terr]

   I need a doctor j'ai besoin d'un docteur [jay ber-zwān . . .]

   YOU MAY HEAR . . .

   est-ce que vous avez déjà eu ça? *have you had this before?*

   où est-ce que ça vous fait mal? *where does it hurt?*

   est-ce que vous prenez des médicaments? *are you taking any drugs?*

   prenez-en deux, trois fois par jour/aux heures des repas *take two, three times a day/at meal times*

document un document [dohkoo-mōn]

dog un chien [shee-yān]

don't *see* not

   don't! non! [nōn]

door la porte [pohrt]

dosage la dose [dohz]
douane Customs
double double [doobl]
   double room une chambre pour deux
   [shōnbr poor der]
   double whisky un double whisky
douche shower
Dover Douvres [doovr]
down en bas [ōn-bah]
   downstairs au rez-de-chaussée [rayd-shoh-say]
   get down! descendez! [day-sōn-day]
drain *(in street)* un égout [ay-goo]
   (in bathroom) le tuyau d'écoulement [twee-yoh
   daykool-mōn]
drawing pin une punaise [poo-nayz]
dress une robe [rohb]
   I'm not dressed je ne suis pas habillé
   [. . . pahz-ahbee-yay]
» *TRAVEL TIP: sizes*

UK	10	12	14	16	18	20
France	38	40	42	44	46	48

   dressing gown la robe de chambre [. . . shōnbr]
dressing *(on wound)* un pansement [pōns-mōn]
   (in salad etc) l'assaisonnement [ahsay-zon-mōn]
drink *(verb)* boire [bwahr]
   something to drink quelque chose à boire
   would you like a drink? désirez-vous [dayzee-ray
   voo] boire quelque chose?
   I don't drink je ne bois pas d'alcool [jer ner bwah pah
   dal-kol]
   is the water drinkable? est-ce que l'eau est potable?
   [esker loh ay poh-tahbl]
drive conduire [kōn-dweer]
   I've been driving all day j'ai roulé [roo-lay] toute la
   journée
   I was driving c'est moi qui conduisais [kōndwee-zay]
   driver le conducteur [kōndook-terr]
   (taxi) le chauffeur [shoh-ferr]
driving licence le permis [pair-mee] de conduire
» *TRAVEL TIP: driving in France pay attention to
'priorité': as a rule cars coming from the right have right
of way unless you are in a 'passage protégé', when you
have the right of way; always have your licence ready*

droguerie *hardware shop*
drown: he's drowning il se noie [eel ser nwah]
drug un médicament [maydee-kah-mōn]
  (narcotic etc) la drogue [drog]
  he is on drugs il prend [prōn] des médicaments
drunk ivre [eevr]
dry *(adjective)* sec (sèche) [sek, sesh]
  (verb) sécher [say-shay]
  dry-clean nettoyer à sec [naytwah-yay ah sek]
  dry-cleaner's une teinturerie [tāntoor-ree]
due: when is the bus due? quand est-ce que le bus doit
  arriver? [kōnt esker ler boos dwaht ahree-vay]
during pendant [pōn-dōn]
dust la poussière [poos-yair]
duty-free hors taxe [ohr-tax]
  duty-free shop une boutique hors taxe
dynamo la dynamo [deenah-moh]
each chaque [shahk]
  can we have one each? est-ce que nous pouvons en
  avoir un chacun? [. . . ōn nah-vwahr ān shah-kān]
  how much are they each? combien est-ce qu'ils sont
  la pièce? [kōnb-yān eskeel sōn lah pee-yes]
ear l'oreille [oh-ray]
  I have earache j'ai des douleurs [doo-lerr] à l'oreille
early tôt [toh]
  we want to leave a day earlier nous voulons partir
  un jour plus tôt [noo voo-lōn pahr-teer ān joor ploo toh]
earring une boucle d'oreille [bookl doh-ray]
east l'est [est]
easy facile [fah-seel]
Easter Pâques [pahk]
  at Easter à Pâques
  Easter Monday le lundi [lān-dee] de Pâques
eat manger [mōn-jay]
  something to eat quelque chose [kel-ker shohz] à
  manger
eau potable *drinking water*
egg un oeuf [erf]
Eire la République d'Irlande [. . . eer-lōnd]
either: either this one or that one ou celui-ci ou
  celui-là [oo serlwee-see oo serlwee-lah]
  I don't like either aucun des deux ne me plaît
  [oh-kān day der . . .]

either would do ou l'un ou l'autre fera l'affaire
[oo lan oo lohtr . . .]
elastic élastique [aylass-teek]
  an elastic band un élastique
elbow le coude [kood]
electric électrique [aylek-treek]
  electric blanket une couverture chauffante
  [koovair-toor shoh-font]
  electric fire un radiateur électrique [rahd-yah-ter
  aylek-trik]
electricity l'électricité [aylek-tree-see-tay]
» TRAVEL TIP: 220v the rule but 110v also in use: do
  check; 2-pin plugs widely used, also 3-pin plug; get an
  adaptor before you go, or buy a 'prise électrique' in a
  local supermarket
électro-ménager electrical appliances
elegant élégant [aylay-gon]
else: something else quelque chose d'autre
  [kelker-shoz dohtr]
  somebody else quelqu'un d'autre [kelkan dohtr]
  somewhere else ailleurs [ah-yerr]
  who/what else? qui/quoi d'autre? [kee, kwah dohtr]
  or else . . . sinon . . . [see-non]
embarrassing embarrassant [onbah-rah-son]
embarrassed gêné [jay-nay]
embassy l'ambassade [onbah-sad]
emergency une urgence [oor-jons]
  help me please aidez-moi s'il vous plaît
  [ayday-mwah see voo play]
» TRAVEL TIP: emergency numbers on all telephone
  dials; 'pompiers' fire brigade; 'Police Secours' police
empty vide [veed]
enclose: I enclose with my letter . . . je joins à ma
  lettre . . . [jer jwan ah ma laitr]
end la fin [fan]
  when does it end? quand-est-ce que ça finit? [kon
  tesker sah fee-nee]
enfants children
engaged occupé [ohkoo-pay]
  (to be married) fiancé [fee-on-say]
engine le moteur [moh-terr]
  engine trouble des ennuis mécaniques [on-nwee
  maykah-neek]

England l'Angleterre [ŏngler-tair]
  English anglais [ŏn-glay]
  Englishman un Anglais
  Englishwoman une Anglaise [ŏn-glayz]
enjoy: I enjoyed it very much j'ai beaucoup aimé [jay
  boh-koo ay-may]
  I enjoyed the meal j'ai très bien mangé
  [jay trayb-yăn mŏn-jay]
enlargement *(photo)* un agrandissement
  [ahgrŏn-dees-mŏn]
enormous énorme [ay-norm]
enough assez [ah-say]
  that's not big enough ce n'est pas assez grand
  I don't have enough money je n'ai pas assez
  d'argent
  thank you, that's enough merci, ça suffit [soo-fee]
enquiries office le bureau des renseignements [booroh
  day rŏnsayn-mŏn]
entertainment *(shows etc)* les attractions
  [ahtraks-yŏn]
entrance l'entrée [ŏn-tray]
entry l'entrée [ŏn-tray]
  entry permit un laisser-passer [laysay-pah-say]
envelope une enveloppe [ŏnv-lop]
equipment *(sport etc)* le matériel [mahtayr-yel]
error une erreur [ay-rer]
escalator un escalier roulant [eskahl-yay roo-lŏn]
especially spécialement [spays-yahl-mŏn]
essential essentiel [aysŏns-yel]
Europe l'Europe [er-rop]
  European européen [er-roh-pay-ăn]
evacuate évacuer [ayvah-kooay]
even même [maim]
evening le soir [swahr]
  in the evening le soir
  evening dress la robe de soirée [rob der swah-ray]
ever: have you ever been to . . .? est-ce que vous êtes
  déjà allé à . . .? [esker voo zait day-jah ahlay ah]
every chaque [shahk]
  every day chaque jour [shahk joor]
  everyone chacun [shah-kŭn], tous *(plural)* [toos]
  everything tout [too]
  everywhere partout [pahr-too]

evidence: to give evidence témoigner [taymwahn-yay]

exact exact [ayg-zakt]

example un exemple [ayg-zōnpl]
  for example par exemple

excellent excellent [ayksay-lōn]

except: except me à part moi [ah-par . . .]

excess *(insurance)* la franchise [frōn-sheez]
  excess baggage un excédent de bagages [ayksay-dōn der bah-gahj]

exchange *(money)* le change [shōnj]
  (telephone) le central [sōntral]
  exchange rate le taux de change [toh der shōnj]

excursion une excursion [exkoors-yōn]

excuse me pardon Monsieur (*or* Madame, Mademoiselle) [pahr-dōn mers-yer, mah-dam, mahder-mwah-zel]

exhaust *(car)* le tuyau d'échappement [twee-oh dayshap-mōn]

exhausted épuisé [aypwee-zay]

exhibition une exposition [expoh-zees-yōn]

exhibitor un exposant [expoh-zōn]

exit la sortie [sohr-tee]

expect: she's expecting elle attend un bébé [el ah-tōn ān bay-bay]
  I'm expected je suis attendu [jer swee ahtōn-doo]

expenses les dépenses [day-pōns]
  it's on expenses ça va sur la note de frais [sah vah soor lah not der fray]

expensive cher [shair]

expert un spécialiste [spays-yah-leest]

explain expliquer [explee-kay]

export exporter [expohr-tay]

exposure: 24 exposure film un film de vingt-quatre poses [. . . pohz]
  exposure meter un posemètre [pohz-maitr]

express: I'd like to send it express j'aimerais l'envoyer par exprès [jaym-ray lōnvwah-yay pahr ex-pres]

extra: is it extra? est-ce que c'est en supplément? [esker say ōn sooplay-mōn]
  an extra blanket une couverture de plus [oon koovair-toor der ploos]

eye l'oeil [er-ee]
  the eyes les yeux [yer]
  eye bath une lotion [lohs-yōn] pour les yeux
  eyeshadow le fard à paupières
  [fahr ah pohp-yair]
  eye witness un témoin oculaire [tay-mwān
  ohkoo-lair]
fabric un tissu [tee-soo]
face le visage [vee-zahj]
factory une fabrique [fah-brik]
Fahrenheit *see* **centigrade**
faint: she's fainted elle s'est évanouie [el sayt
  ayvah-nwee]
fair une foire [fwahr]
  that's not fair ce n'est pas juste [ser nay pah joost]
faithfully *see* **letter**
fake faux (fausse) [foh, fohs]
fall tomber [tōn-bay]
  he's fallen il est tombé
false faux (fausse) [foh, fohs]
  false teeth un dentier [dōnt-yay]
family la famille [fah-mee]
  do you have any family? est-ce que vous avez des
  enfants? [esker voo zah-vay day zōnfōn]
fan *(in car, room etc)* le ventilateur [vōntee-lah-terr]
  (supporter) un supporter [soopohr-tair]
  fan belt la courroie de ventilateur [koo-rwah . . .]
far loin [lwān]
  is it far? est-ce que c'est loin? [esker say lwān]
  how far is it? c'est à quelle distance d'ici? [say ah kel
  dees-tōns dee-see]
fare *(travel)* le prix du billet [pree doo bee-yay]
  half fare le demi-tarif [der-mee tah-reef]
  full fare le plein tarif [plān . . .]
farm une ferme [fairm]
farther plus loin [ploo lwān]
fashion la mode [mod]
  fashion shop une boutique de mode
fast *(adjective)* rapide [rah-peed]
  don't speak so fast ne parlez pas si vite [ner pahr-lay
  pah see veet]
fat gros [groh]
  (on meat) du gras [grah]

father: my father mon père [pair]
fathom une brasse *(1.83 m)*
fault un défaut [day-foh]
  there's a fault c'est défectueux [dayfek-too-er]
  it's not my fault ce n'est pas de ma faute [ser nay pahd mah foht]
favourite préféré [prayfay-ray]
February: in February en février [fayvree-ay]
fed-up: I'm fed-up j'en ai assez [jōn nay ah-say]
fee: what's the fee? combien ça coûte? [kōnb-yān sah koot]
feel: I feel cold/hot j'ai froid/chaud [jay frwah, shoh]
  I don't feel well je ne me sens pas bien [jern mer sōn pah bee-yān]
  I feel ill je me sens mal [jerm sōn mal]
  I feel sick j'ai mal au coeur [jay mal oh kerr]
  I feel like *(I want)* j'ai envie de [jay ōn-vee der]
felt-tip pen un stylo-feutre [steeloh-fertr]
femmes women
fermé closed
ferry le ferry-boat [fairee-boht]
festival un festival [festee-val]
fetch: will you come and fetch me? est-ce que vous pouvez venir me chercher? [esker voo poovay ver-neer mer shair-shay]
  could you go and fetch ...? est-ce que vous pouvez aller chercher ...?
fever la fièvre [fee-yaivr]
  I am feverish j'ai de la fièvre [jay ...]
few: few people peu de gens [per der jōn]
  a few days quelques jours [kel-ker joor]
  only a few seulement quelques uns [serl-mōn kelker-zān]
fiancé: my fiancé mon fiancé [fee-yōn-say]
  my fiancée ma fiancée
fiddle: it's a fiddle c'est malhonnête [maloh-nait]
field un champ [shōn]
fig une figue [fig]
fight: there's been a fight il y a eu une bagarre [eelyahoo oon bah-gahr]
figure *(digit)* un chiffre [sheefr]
  I'm watching my figure je surveille ma ligne [jer soor-vay mah leen]

fill remplir [rōn-pleer]
  fill her up faites le plein [fait ler plān]
  do I have to fill in a form? est-ce que je dois remplir un formulaire?
  [esker jer dwah rōn-pleerr ān fohrmoo-lair]
fillet un filet [fee-lay]
filling *(in tooth)* un plombage [plōn-bahj]
film un film
  I would like a 35 mm film j'aimerais un film 24 × 36
  [jaym-ray ān film vānt-kat trōnt-sees]
  a colour/b & w film un film couleur/noir et blanc
  [. . . koo-lerr, nwahr ay blōn]
  a 20 exposure film un film de vingt poses
  [. . . der vān pohz]
filter un filtre [feeltr]
  I was in the filter lane j'étais dans la voie de sortie
  [jay-tay dōn lah vwah der sohr-tee]
find trouver [troo-vay]
  if you find it si vous le (la) trouvez [see voo ler troo-vay]
  I've found a . . . j'ai trouvé un . . . [jay . . .]
fine: **the weather is fine** il fait beau temps [eel fay boh tōn]
  a 50 francs fine une amende de cinquante francs [oon ah-mōnd der . . .]
  OK, that's fine d'accord, ça va bien [dah-kor sah vah bee-yān]
finger le doigt [dwah]
  fingernail un ongle [ōngl]
finish finir [fee-neer]
  I haven't finished je n'ai pas fini [jer nay pah fee-nee]
fire un feu [fer]
  (blaze: house on fire etc) un incendie [ānsōn-dee]
  (heater) un radiateur [rahd-yah-terr]
  fire! au feu! [oh fer]
  can we light a fire here? est-ce qu'on peut faire du feu ici? [eskōn per fair doo fer ee-see]
  call the fire brigade appelez les pompiers [ap-lay lay pōnp-yay]
  » TRAVEL TIP: *the fire brigade number 'pompiers' is on all telephone dials*
  it's not firing *(car)* il y a un défaut à l'allumage [eelyah ān day-foh ah lahloo-mahj]

fire extinguisher un extincteur [ex-tãnk-terr]
fireworks un feu d'artifice [fer dahrtee-fees]
firm une entreprise [õntrer-preez]
first premier [prerm-yay]
  I was first j'étais le premier
  first aid les premiers secours [. . . ser-koor]
  first aid kit une trousse [troos] de premiers secours
  first name le prénom [pray-nõn]
fish du poisson [pwah-sõn]
fishmonger's une poissonnerie [pwahson-ree]
fishing la pêche [paish]
  fishing rod une canne [kan] à pêche
» *TRAVEL TIP: if you want to go fishing you will need a*
  special permit, 'le permis de pêche'; enquire at the
  'syndicat d'initiative'
fit *(healthy)* en bonne condition physique [õn bonn
  kõndees-yõn fee-zeek]
  it doesn't fit me ça ne me va pas [sann mer vah pah]
fix: can you fix it? *(repair)* est-ce que vous pouvez le
  réparer? [esker voo poo-vay ler raypah-ray]
  (arrange) est-ce que vous pouvez arranger ça?
  [. . . ahrõnjay sah]
fizzy mousseux [moo-ser]
flag un drapeau [drah-poh]
flannel un gant de toilette [gõn der twah-let]
flash *(photo)* un flash
  flashcube une ampoule de flash [õn-pool . . .]
flat plat [plah]
  (noun) un appartement [ahpahr-ter-mõn]
  I've got a flat *(tyre)* j'ai un pneu à plat
  [jay ãn pner . . .]
  can you repair a flat? est-ce que vous pouvez réparer
  une crevaison? [esker voo poovay raypah-ray oon
  krervay-zõn]
flavour la saveur [sah-verr]
fleas des puces [poos]
flies *(on trousers)* la braguette [brah-get]
flight un vol
flippers des palmes [pahlm]
float flotter
floor: on which floor? à quel étage? [ah kel ay-tahj]
  the ground floor le rez-de-chaussée [rayd-
  .shoh-say]

the top floor le dernier étage [dairn-yay . . .]
on the floor par terre [par tair]
flowers des fleurs [flerr]
flu la grippe [grip]
fly *(insect)* la mouche [moosh]
we flew here nous sommes venus en avion [noo som ver-noo ōnn ahv-yōn]
foggy: it's foggy il y a du brouillard [eelyah doo broo-yahr]
fold plier [plee-yay]
follow suivre [sweevr]
food la nourriture [nooree-toor]
food store un magasin d'alimentation [mahgah-zān dahleemōn-tahs-yōn]
food poisoning une intoxication alimentaire [āntohksee-kahs-yōn ahlee-mōn-tair]
foot le pied [pee-yay]
» *TRAVEL TIP: 1 foot = 30.1 cm = 0.3 m*
football le football
for pour
we've been here for a week nous sommes ici depuis une semaine [noo som zee-see der-pwee . . .]
forbidden interdit [āntair-dee]
foreign étranger [aytrōn-jay]
foreigner un étranger
forest une forêt [foh-ray]
forget oublier [ooblee-yay]
I've forgotten . . . j'ai oublié . . . [jay . . .]
don't forget n'oubliez pas [nooblee-yay pah]
fork une fourchette [foor-shet]
form un formulaire [fohrmoo-lair]
formal officiel [ohfees-yel]
fortnight: for a fortnight pour deux semaines [. . . der ser-mayn]
fortunate: we were fortunate nous avons eu de la chance [noo zah-vōn oo der lah shōns]
fortunately heureusement [er-rerz-mōn]
forward en avant [ōn nah-vōn]
could you forward my mail? est-ce que vous pouvez faire suivre mon courrier? [. . . fair sweevr mōn koor-yay]
here is a forwarding address voici l'adresse où envoyer le courrier [lah-dress oo ōnvwah-yay . . .]

foundation cream un fond de teint [fon der tan]
fountain une fontaine [fon-tain]
fracture une fracture [frak-toor]
fragile fragile [frah-jeel]
franc un franc [fron]
   Swiss francs des francs suisses [. . . sweess]
   Belgian francs des francs belges [. . . belj]
France la France [frons]
free libre [leebr]
freezer un congélateur [konjay-lah-terr]
French français [fron-say]
   Frenchman un Français
   Frenchwoman une Française [fron-sayz]
   I don't speak French je ne parle pas français [jer ner
   pahrl pah fron-say]
fresh frais (fraîche) [fray, fraish]
freshen up: I'd like to go and freshen up
   j'aimerais faire un peu de toilette [jaym-ray fair an per
   der twah-let]
Friday vendredi [vondrer-dee]
fridge un frigo [free-goh]
fried frit [free]
   fried egg un oeuf sur le plat [an nerf soor ler plah]
   nothing fried pas de fritures [pah der free-toor]
friend un ami [ah-mee]
friendly sympathique [sanpah-teek]
from de [der]
   where is it from? d'où est-ce que ça vient? [doo esker
   sah vee-yan]
front: in front (of) devant [der-von]
frost le gel [jel]
   frostbite des gelures [jer-loor]
frozen gelé [jer-lay]
   frozen food des aliments surgelés [ahlee-
   mon soorjer-lay]
fruit des fruits [frwee]
   fruit juice un jus de fruits [joo der frwee]
   fruit salad une macédoine de fruits
   [mahsay-dwahn]
fry frire [freer]
   frying pan une poêle [pwahl]
full plein [plan]
fumeurs: non-fumeurs no smoking

fun: it's fun c'est amusant [sayt ahmoo-zon]
  we had fun nous nous sommes bien amusés [noo noo som bee-yan ahmoo-zay]
funny drôle [drohl]
furniture les meubles [merbl]
further plus loin [ploo lwan]
fuse un fusible [foo-zeebl]
fuss: I don't want any fuss je ne veux pas d'histoires [jer ner ver pah dees-twahr]
future: in future à l'avenir [ah lahv-neer]
gale une tempête [ton-pet]
gallon un gallon [gah-lon]
  » *TRAVEL TIP: 1 gallon = 4.55 litres*
gallstone un calcul biliaire [kal-kool beel-yair]
gambling: I like gambling j'aime le jeu [jaym ler jer]
game un jeu [jer]
gammon du jambon [jon-bon]
garage un garage [gah-rahj]
  » *TRAVEL TIP: ask for 'un devis' (estimate), 'une facture détaillée' (itemized bill), 'la durée des réparations' (estimated time for repairs); avoid M-way garages whenever possible*
garden un jardin [jahr-dan]
garlic l'ail [as 'eye']
gas le gaz [gahz]
  (petrol) de l'essence [ay-sons]
  gas cylinder une bouteille de gaz [boo-tay . . .]
gasket un joint [jwan]
gauge une jauge [johj]
gear *(in car)* la vitesse [vee-tess]
  (equipment) le matériel [mahtayr-yel]
  in 1st gear en première vitesse [prerm-yair . . .]
  gearbox trouble des ennuis avec la boîte de vitesses [dayz-on-nwee ah-vek lah bwaht der vee-tess]
  gear lever le levier de vitesses [lerv-yay]
  I can't get it into gear je n'arrive pas à mettre la vitesse [jer nah-reev pah ah maitr . . .]
gentleman: the gentleman here told me . . . ce monsieur m'a dit . . . [ser mers-yer mah dee]
gents les toilettes (pour messieurs) [lay twah-let poor mays-yer]
genuine véritable [vayree-tahbl]
German allemand [al-mon]

Germany l'Allemagne [al-mann]
gesture un geste [jest]
» *TRAVEL TIP: the French use their hands more than the British do when they speak; be prepared to shake hands as often as required*
get: will you get me a . . .? est-ce que vous pouvez me chercher un . . .? [esker voo poovay mer shair-shay]
  how do I get to . . .? comment est-ce qu'on peut aller à . . .? [koh-mōn eskōn per ah-lay ah]
  we got here last night nous sommes arrivés hier soir [noo somz ahreevay . . .]
  when can I get it back? quand est-ce que je peux le ravoir? [kōntesker jer per ler rah-vwahr]
  when do we get back? quand est-ce que nous rentrons? [. . . rōn-trōn]
  get down descendre [day-sōndr]
  when do I get off? où est-ce que je dois descendre? [wesker jer dwah day-sōndr]
  I can't get in je ne peux pas entrer [jern per pah ōn-tray]
  get out sortir [sohr-teer]
  I get up at 7 je me lève à sept heures [jer mer laiv . . .]
gin du gin [djeen]
  gin and tonic un gin and tonic
girl une fille [fee]
  my girlfriend mon amie [ah-mee]
  NB 'fille' also means 'daughter'; 'jeune fille' [jern . . .] is used of unmarried girl
gîtes ruraux *self-catering accommodation*
gîtes d'étape *dormitory accommodation (for ramblers etc)*
give donner [doh-nay]
  will you give me . . .? est-ce que vous pouvez me donner . . .? [esker voo poovay mer doh-nay]
  can you give me back . . .? est-ce que vous pouvez me rendre . . .? [. . . mer rōndr]
glad: I'm glad (to . . .) je suis content (de . . .) [jer swee kōn-tōn . . .]
glass un verre [vair]
  glass of water/of wine un verre d'eau/de vin [vairdoh, vairder-vān]
glasses: my glasses mes lunettes [loo-net]
gloves des gants [gōn]

glue de la colle [kol]
go aller [ah-lay]
    he's/they are going there on Sunday il y va/ils y
    vont dimanche [eel ee vah, eel zee v$\overline{on}$]
    where are you going? où allez-vous?
    [oo ah-lay voo]
    I'm/we are going there tomorrow j'y vais/nous y
    allons demain [jee vay, noo zee ah-l$\overline{on}$ . . .]
    he's gone il est parti [eelay pahr-tee]
    we went to Italy last year nous sommes allés en
    Italie l'année dernière [noo somz ah-lay . . .]
    can I have a go? est-ce que je peux essayer? [esker jer
    per aysay-yay]
    my car won't go ma voiture ne part pas [mah
    vwah-toor ner pahr pah]
    when does the bus go? quand est-ce que le bus part?
    [k$\overline{on}$t esker ler boos pahr]
    go down descendre [day-s$\overline{on}$dr]; **go in** entrer
    [$\overline{on}$-tray]; **go on** continuer [k$\overline{on}$tee-nway]; **go out**
    sortir [sohr-teer]; **go up** monter [m$\overline{on}$-tay]
goal un but [boot]
goat une chèvre [shaivr]
    goat's cheese du fromage de chèvre [froh-mahj . . .]
God Dieu [dee-yer]
goggles des lunettes protectrices [loo-net
  prohtek-trees]
gold: a gold chain une chaînette en or [shay-net $\overline{on}$n
  ohr]
    YOU MAY HEAR . . .
    c'est plaqué or *it's gold plated*
golf le golf [gohlf]
    golf course un terrain [tay-r$\overline{an}$] de golf
good bon [b$\overline{on}$]
    good! très bien! [tray bee-y$\overline{an}$]
    be good! soyez sage! [swah-yay sahj]
    good luck! bonne chance! [bonn sh$\overline{on}$s]
    good morning, good afternoon bonjour (Monsieur
    or Madame *or* Mademoiselle) [b$\overline{on}$-joor mers-yer,
    mah-dam, mad-mwah-zel]
    good evening bonsoir (Monsieur *or* Madame *or*
    Mademoiselle) [b$\overline{on}$-swahr . . .]
    good night bonne nuit! [bonn nwee]
    Good Friday le Vendredi saint [v$\overline{on}$drer-dee s$\overline{an}$]

....

goodbye au revoir! [oh rer-vwahr]
gooseberries des groseilles à maquereau [groh-zay ah mak-roh]
gramme un gramme [gram]
» *TRAVEL TIP: 100 grammes = 3½ oz*
grand grand [grōn]
  my grandfather mon grand-père [grōn-pair]
  my grandmother ma grand-mère [grōn-mair]
  my grandchildren mes petits-enfants
  my grandson mon petit-fils [pertee-fees]
  my granddaughter ma petite-fille [perteet-fee]
grape un raisin [ray-zān]
  grapes du raisin
grapefruit un pamplemousse [pōnpler-moos]
  grapefruit juice un jus [joo] de pamplemousse
grass l'herbe [airb]
grateful: I'm very grateful to you je vous suis très reconnaissant [jer voo swee tray rerkoh-nay-sōn]
gratuit free
gravy la sauce [sohs]
grease *(noun)* la graisse [grays]
  (verb) graisser [gray-say]
  greasy graisseux [gray-ser]
great grand [grōn]
  great! parfait! [pahr-fay]
green vert [vair]
greengrocer's un marchand de fruits et légumes [mahr-shōn der frweez ay lay-goom]
  green card la carte verte [kahrt vairt]
grey gris [gree]
grilled grillé [gree-yay]
grocer's une épicerie [aypees-ree]
ground: on the ground par terre [par tair]
  on the ground floor au rez-de-chaussée [rayd-shoh-say]
group un groupe [groop]
  our group leader notre chef [shef] de groupe
  I'm with the English group je suis [jer swee] avec le groupe des Anglais
guarantee une garantie [gahrōn-tee]
guest un invité [ānvee-tay]
  (in hotel) un client [klee-yōn]
  guesthouse une pension [pōns-yōn]

guide un guide [gheed]
  a guidebook in English un guide en anglais [. . . ānn on-glay]
  guided tour une visite guidée [vee-zeet ghee-day]
guilty coupable [koo-pahbl]
guitar: do you play the guitar? est-ce que vous jouez de la guitare? [esker voo jway der lah ghee-tahr]
gums les gencives [jōn-seev]
gun un revolver [rayvol-vair]
  (rifle) un fusil [foo-zee]
gynaecologist un gynécologue [jeenay-koh-log]
hair les cheveux [sher-ver]
  hairbrush une brosse à cheveux [bross . . .]
  haircut une coupe de cheveux [koop . . .]
  where can I get a haircut? où est-ce que je peux me faire couper les cheveux? [wesker jer per mer fair koo-pay lay sher-ver]
  is there a (ladies') hairdresser's here? est-ce qu'il y a un coiffeur (pour dames) ici? [. . . kwah-ferr poor dahm]
  hairdrier un sèche-cheveux [sesh sher-ver]
half la moitié [mwaht-yay]
  a half portion une demi-portion [der-mee pohrs-yōn]
  half an hour une demi-heure [der-mee err]
ham du jambon [jōn-bōn]
hamburger un hamburger [ōnberr-gherr]
hammer un marteau [mahr-toh]
hand la main [mān]
  handbag un sac à main
  handbrake le frein à main [frān . . .]
handkerchief un mouchoir [moo-shwahr]
handle la poignée [pwahn-yay]
hand luggage les bagages à main [bah-gahj ah mān]
handmade fait à la main [fay ah lah mān]
handsome beau (belle) [boh, bel]
hanger un cintre [sāntr]
hangover la gueule de bois [gerl der bwah]
happen: what happened? qu'est-ce qui s'est passé? [keskee say pah-say]
  I don't know how it happened je ne sais pas comment c'est arrivé [. . . koh-mōn sayt ahree-vay]
  what's happening? qu'est-ce qui se passe? [keskee ser pass]

happy heureux [er-rer]
harbour le port [pohr]
hard dur [door]
  hard-boiled egg un oeuf dur [erf door]
  push hard poussez fort [. . . fohr]
harm: can it do (him) any harm? est-ce que ça peut
  (lui) faire du mal? [esker sah per lwee fair doo mal]
hat un chapeau [shah-poh]
hate: I hate . . . je déteste . . . [day-test]
have avoir [ah-vwahr]
  I have j'ai [jay]
  he/she has il/elle a [eel, el ah]
  we have nous avons [nooz ah-vōn]
  they have ils/elles ont [eelz ōn, elz ōn]
  do you have any cigars/a map? est-ce que vous avez
  des cigares/une carte? [esker vooz ah-vay . . .]
  can I have some water? est-ce que je peux avoir de
  l'eau? [esker jer per ah-vwahr . . .]
  I have to leave tomorrow je dois partir demain [jer
  dwah . . .]
  we have to . . . nous devons . . . [noo der-vōn]
hayfever le rhume des foins [room day fwān]
he il [eel]
head la tête [tait]
  headache un mal de tête [mal der tait]
  I have a (bad) headache j'ai (très) mal à la tête [jay
  tray mal . . .]
  headlights les phares [fahr]
» *TRAVEL TIP: flashing headlights doesn't normally
  mean 'after you'!*
  head waiter le maître d'hôtel [meitr doh-tel]
  head wind un vent contraire [kōn-trair]
health la santé [sōn-tay]
  your health! à votre santé! [ah vohtr sōn-tay]
  healthy en bonne santé [ōn bon . . .]
hear entendre [ōn-tōndr]
  I can't hear je n'entends pas [jer nōn-tōn pah]
  hearing aid un appareil acoustique [ahpah-ray
  ahkoos-teek]
heart le coeur [kerr]
  heart attack une crise cardiaque [kreez kard-yak]
heat la chaleur [shah-lerr]
  heat stroke un coup de chaleur [koo der . . .]

heater un radiateur [rahd-yah-terr]
heating le chauffage [shoh-fahj]
  central heating le chauffage central
  [shoh-fahj sōn-trahl]
heavy lourd [loor]
heel le talon [tah-lōn]
  can you put new heels on these? est-ce que vous
  pouvez me refaire les talons de ces chaussures?
  [. . . mer rer-fair lay tah-lōn der say shoh-soor]
height la hauteur [oh-terr]
  I'm 5 ft 6 je mesure un mètre soixante cinq [jer
  mer-zoor ān maitr . . .]
hello bonjour [bōn-joor]
help aider [ay-day]
  can you help me? est-ce que vous pouvez m'aider?
  [esker voo poo-vay may-day]
  can anybody help? est-ce que quelqu'un [kel-kān]
  peut m'aider (or nous aider)?
  thanks for your help merci de votre aide [mair-see
  der vohtr aid]
  help! au secours! [oh ser-koor]
her: **I know her** je la connais [. . . lah . . .]
  give her . . . donnez-lui . . . [. . . lwee]
  give it back to her rendez-le lui
  it's her c'est elle [sayt el]
  her bag *etc see* **his**
here ici [ee-see]
high haut [oh]
  higher up plus haut [ploo oh]
  high chair une chaise haute [shayz oht]
hill une colline [koh-leen]
  (on road) une côte [koht]
him: **I know him** je le connais [. . . ler . . .]
  give him . . . donnez-lui . . . [. . . lwee]
  give it to him donnez-le lui
  it's him c'est lui
hire *see* **rent**
his, her, its son [sōn], sa [sah], *(plural)* ses [say]
  it's his (her) bag, it's his (hers) c'est son sac, c'est le
  sien [. . . ler see-yān]
  it's his (her) car, it's (his) hers c'est sa voiture, c'est
  la sienne [. . . lah see-enn] *(in the plural* les siens, les
  siennes)

....

hit: he hit me il m'a frappé [. . . frah-pay]
   the car hit him la voiture l'a heurté [. . . err-tay]
hitch-hike faire de l'auto-stop
   [fair der loh-toh-stop]
   hitch-hiker un auto-stoppeur [oh-toh stoh-perr]
hold tenir [ter-neer]
   hold this tenez ça [ter-nay . . .]
   I'm holding it je le tiens [. . . tee-yān]
hole un trou [troo]
holiday les vacances [vah-kōns]
   I'm on holiday je suis en vacances [jer sweez ōn . . .]
Holland la Hollande [oh-lōnd]
   in Holland en Hollande
home: at home chez moi [shay mwah]
   (back in Britain) chez nous [shay noo]
   I'm homesick j'ai le mal du pays [jay ler mal doo
   pay-yee]
   we must go home nous devons rentrer
hommes men
honest honnête [oh-net]
   honestly? vraiment? [vray-mōn]
honey du miel [mee-yel]
honeymoon: our honeymoon notre lune de miel
   [nohtr loon der mee-yel]
hope: I hope that . . . j'espère que . . . [jes-pair ker]
   I hope so/not j'espère que oui/non
horizon l'horizon [ohree-zōn]
horn *(car)* l'avertisseur [ahvair-tee-serr]
   I sounded my horn j'ai klaxonné [jay klaxoh-nay]
horrible horrible [oh-reebl]
hors d'oeuvre les hors d'oeuvre [ohr dervr]
horse un cheval [sher-val]
   horse-racing les courses de chevaux [koors der
   sher-voh]
hose un tuyau (souple) [twee-yoh soopl]
hospital un hôpital [ohpee-tal]
   will he have to go to hospital? est-ce qu'il faut
   l'hospitaliser? [. . . lospee-tah-lee-zay]
» *TRAVEL TIP: free of charge in France provided you
  belong to a national insurance scheme in Britain; some
  'cliniques' (private hospitals) are 'conventionnées', i.e.
  covered by reciprocal health agreements; get the specia
  form from the Post Office*

host l'hôte [oht]
 hostess l'hôtesse [oh-tess]
hot chaud [shoh]
 (spiced) fort [fohr]
hotel un hôtel [oh-tel]
» *TRAVEL TIP: price is per room unless specified
 otherwise; breakfast extra; nominal charge for children
 sharing the room; tariffs must be displayed inside the
 room; there are plenty of inexpensive (one- and
 two-star) hotels in most towns; you may be asked to
 leave your passport at reception when booking in*
hotplate une plaque chauffante [plak shoh-fōnt]
hot-water bottle une bouillotte [boo-yot]
hour une heure [err]
house une maison [may-zōn]
housewife une ménagère [maynah-jair]
how comment [koh-mōn]
 how are you?, how do you do? comment allez-vous?
 [koh-mōnt ah-lay voo]
 how many?, how much? combien [kōmb-yān]
 how much is it? combien ça coûte?
 [kōnb-yān sah koot]
 how many days? combien de jours?
 how long does it take to . . .? combien de temps
 est-ce qu'il faut pour . . .? [kōnb-yān der tōn eskeel foh
 poor]
 how long have you been here? vous êtes ici depuis
 combien de temps? [vooz ayt ee-see der-pwee kōnb-yān
 der tōn]
 how often do the buses go? il y a des bus tous les
 combien? [eelyah day boos too lay kōnb-yān]
 how high/long/wide/deep is . . .? quelle est la
 hauteur/longueur/largeur/profondeur de . . .? [kel ay
 lah oh-ter, lōn-gher, lahr-jer, prohfōn-der der]
hull la coque [kok]
humid humide [oo-meed]
humour: you need a sense of humour il faut avoir le
 sens de l'humour [eel foht ah-vwahr ler sōns der
 loo-moor]
hundredweight *1 cwt = 50.8 kilos*
hungry: I'm hungry j'ai faim [jay fān]
 I'm not hungry je n'ai pas faim [jer nay pah fān]
hurry: I'm in a hurry je suis pressé [jer swee pray-say]

....

please hurry! dépêchez-vous [daypay-shay-voo]
hurt blesser [blay-say]
 I hurt myself je me suis fait mal [jer mer swee fay
 mal]
 it hurts here ça fait mal ici [sah fay mal ee-see]
 my leg/arm hurts j'ai mal à la jambe/au bras [jay mal
 ah . . .]
husband: my husband mon mari [mōn mah-ree]
I: I am je suis [jer swee]; **I have** j'ai [jay]
ice de la glace [glahs]
 ice-cream une glace
 ice-cream cone un cornet de glace [kor-nay . . .]
 iced-coffee un café glacé [kah-fay glah-say]
 with lots of ice avec beaucoup de glace [ah-vek
 boh-koo . . .]
 ice-rink une patinoire [pahtee-nwahr]
identity papers les papiers d'identité [pahp-yay
 deedōn-tee-tay]
if si [see]
 if we could si nous pouvions [see noo poov-yōn]
ignition l'allumage [ahloo-mahj]
ill malade [mah-lad]
 I feel ill je ne me sens pas bien [jer ner mer sōn pah
 bee-yān]
illegal illégal [eelay-gal]
illegible illisible [eelee-zeebl]
illness une maladie [mahlah-dee]
imitation-leather du simili-cuir [seemee-lee kweer]
immediately tout de suite [toot sweet]
import importer [ānpohr-tay]
 import duty les droits d'importation [drwah
 dānpohr-tahs-yōn]
important: it's very important c'est très important
 [say trayz ānpohr-tōn]
impossible impossible [ānpoh-seebl]
impressive remarquable [rermahr-kahbl]
improve: I want to improve my French je veux
 améliorer mon français
 [jer ver ahmail-yoh-ray mōn . . .]
in dans [dōn]; **in France** en France [ōn . . .]
 in London à Londres [ah . . .]
 in 1982 en 1982 [ōn . . .]
 is he in? est-ce qu'il est là? [eskeelay lah]

inch un pouce [poos]
» *TRAVEL TIP: 1 inch = 2.54 cm*
include inclure [ān-kloor]
  does that include breakfast? est-ce que le petit-déjeuner est compris?
  is it included? est-ce que c'est compris dans le prix?
  is everything included? est-ce que c'est tout compris?
incompetent incompétent [ānkon-pay ton]
inconsiderate: **he was inconsiderate** il a manqué d'égards [eel ah mōn-kay day-gahr]
incontinent incontinent [ānkon-tee-non]
incredible incroyable [ānkrwah-yahbl]
indecent indécent [ānday-son]
independent indépendant [ānday-pon-don]
India l'Inde [ānd]
indicator le clignotant [kleen-yoh-ton]
indigestion une indigestion [āndee-jest-yon]
indoors à l'intérieur [ah lāntayr-yerr]
industry l'industrie [āndoos-tree]
infection une infection [ānfeks-yon]
infectious contagieux [kōntahj-yer]
inflate gonfler [gōn-flay]
inflation l'inflation [ānflahs-yon]
informal simple [sānpl]
  (not official) non-officiel [nonoh-fees-yel]
information: **could you give me some information about...?** est-ce que vous pouvez me renseigner sur [...rōnsayn-yay soor]
  do you have any information in English about...? est-ce que vous avez des informations en anglais sur...? [...dayz ānfohr-mahs-yon ōnn ōn-glay soor]
  information office bureau de renseignements [boo-roh der rōnsayn-yer-mōn]
inhabitants les habitants [ahbee-ton]
injection une piqûre [pee-koor]
injured: **he's been injured** il est blessé [eelay blay-say]
  badly injured gravement blessé [grahv-mōn...]
injury une blessure [blay-soor]
innocent innocent [eenoh-son]
insect un insecte [ān-sekt]

....

insect repellent une crème anti-insecte [krem ōn-tee . . .]

inside à l'intérieur (de . . .) [ah lāntair-yer der]

insist: I insist on it j'y tiens absolument [jee tee-yān apsoh-loo-mōn]

I insist on . . . je veux absolument . . . [jer ver . . .]

insomnia: I suffer from insomnia je souffre d'insomnie [jer soofr dānsom-nee]

instant coffee du café soluble [kah-fay soh-loobl]

instead à la place [ah lah plahs]

instead of au lieu de [oh lee-yer der]

insulating tape de la bande isolante [bōnd eezoh lōnt]

insulation l'isolation [eezoh-lahs-yōn]

insult: he insulted me il m'a insulté [eel mah ānsool-tay]

insurance une assurance [ahsoo-rōns]

which is your insurance company? quelle est votre compagnie d'assurance? [. . . kōnpah-nee . . .]

I'm insured je suis assuré [jer sweez ahsoo-ray]

intelligent intelligent [āntay-lee-jōn]

interdit forbidden

interdit aux piétons no pedestrians

interesting: it's very interesting c'est très intéressant [say trayz āntay-ray-sōn]

international international [āntair-nahs-yoh-nal]

interpret: would you interpret for us? est-ce que vous pouvez nous servir d'interprète? [. . . noo sair-veer dāntair-pret]

into dans [dōn]

introduce: can I introduce . . .? puis-je vous présenter . . .? [pweej voo prayzōn-tay]

invalid un invalide [ānvah-leed]

invalid chair un fauteuil roulant [foh-ter roo-lōn]

invitation une invitation [ānvee-tahs-yōn]

» *TRAVEL TIP: take a present such as flowers or a cake, but never a bottle of wine*

invite inviter [ānvee-tay]

can I invite you out? puis-je vous inviter à sortir avec moi? [pweej vooz ānvee-tay ah sohr-teer ah-vek mwah]

invoice une facture [fak-toor]

Ireland l'Irlande [eer-lōnd]

Irish irlandais [eerlōn-day]

iron *(clothes)* repasser [rerpah-say]
  (noun) un fer à repasser [fair ah . . .]
ironmonger's une quincaillerie [kān-kie-ree]
island une île [eel]
it: put it here mettez le (la) ici
  it is here il (elle) est ici
  where is it? *(a place etc)* où est-ce que c'est? [wesker
  say]; *(a particular object)* où est-ce qu'il (qu'elle) est?
  [weskeel ay]
  give it to me donnez-le (la) moi
  it's him c'est lui [say . . .]
  it's not working ça ne marche pas [sah . . .]
Italy l'Italie [eetah-lee]
  Italian italien [eetahl-yān]
itch: it itches ça démange [sah day-mōnj]
itemize: would you itemize it for me? est-ce que vous
  pouvez me faire une facture détaillée [. . . fak-toor
  daytah-yay]
its *see* **his**
jack un cric [kreek]
jacket une veste [vest]
jam de la confiture [kōnfee-toor]
  traffic jam un embouteillage [ōnboo-tay-yahj]
January: in January en janvier [jōnv-yay]
jaw la mâchoire [mah-shwahr]
jealous jaloux [jah-loo]
jeans des jeans [djeenz]
jellyfish une méduse [may-dooz]
jetty la jetée [jer-tay]
jeweller's une bijouterie [beejoo-tree]
jewellery des bijoux [bee-joo]
job un travail [trah-vie]
join: would you like to join us? est-ce que vous voulez
  venir avec nous? [. . . ver-neer ahvek noo]
joke une plaisanterie [playzōn-tree]
  you must be joking vous plaisantez! [voo
  playzōn-tay]
jours fériés bank holidays
  jour de fermeture closed on . . .
journey un voyage [voh-yahj]
July: in July en juillet [joo-yay]
jumper un pull [pool]
junction un croisement [krwahz-mōn]

June: in June en juin [jwān]
junk du bric à brac [breekah-brak]
just juste [joost]
    he's left just now il vient de partir [eel vee-yān der . . .]
    just there/a little juste là/un petit peu
    not just now pas pour l'instant [pah poor lāns-tōn]
    that's just right ça va très bien [sah vah tray bee-yān]
keen: I'm not keen ça ne me plaît pas beaucoup [sahn mer play pah boh-koo]
keep: can I keep it? est-ce que je peux le garder? [. . . gahr-day]
    keep the change: gardez la monnaie [gahr-day lah moh-nay]
    you didn't keep your promise vous n'avez pas tenu votre promesse [voo nah-vay pah ter-noo vohtr proh-mess]
    it keeps on breaking ça se casse tout le temps [sahs kahs too ler tōn]
    how long does it keep? combien de temps est-ce que ça se garde? [. . . sah ser gahrd]
kettle une bouilloire [boo-ee-wahr]
» *TRAVEL TIP: not a national institution in France; don't necessarily expect to find an electric kettle in a rented flat etc; people tend to boil water in a saucepan*
key une clé [klay]
    the key to no 7 please la clé de la chambre sept, s'il vous plaît
    YOU MAY THEN HEAR . . .
    je vous réveille à quelle heure? *when would you like to be wakened?*
kidneys les reins [rān]
    (food) des rognons [rohn-yōn]
kill tuer [too-ay]
kilo un kilo [kee-loh]
» *TRAVEL TIP: conversion: kilos ÷ 5 × 11 = pounds*

kilos	1	1.5	2	3	5	10	20
lbs	2.2	3.3	4.4	6.6	11	22	44

kilometre un kilomètre [keeloh-maitr]
» *TRAVEL TIP: conversion: km ÷ 8 × 5 = miles*

kilometres	1	5	10	20	50	100
miles	0.62	3.11	6.2	12.4	31	62

kind: that's very kind of you c'est très aimable de
  votre part [say trayz ay-mahbl der vohtr par]
  he's very kind il est très gentil [eel ay tray jōn-tee]
kiss embrasser [ōnbrah-say]
  give me a kiss embrasse-moi [ōnbrahs mwah]
kitchen la cuisine [kwee-zeen]
knee le genou [jer-noo]
knife un couteau [koo-toh]
knitting needle une aiguille à tricoter [ay-gwee ah
  treekoh-tay]
knock: I knocked at the door j'ai frappé à la porte
  [frah-pay . . .]
  there's a knocking noise from the engine il y a le
  moteur qui cogne [eelyah ler moh-terr kee kon]
  he was knocked down by a car il a été renversé par
  une voiture [eel ah ay-tay rōnvair-say par oon
  vwah-toor]
knot un noeud [ner]
know savoir [sah-vwahr]
  I don't know je ne sais pas [jer ner say pah]
  I didn't know je ne savais pas [. . . sah-vay pah]
  we don't know nous ne savons pas [noo ner
  savōn . . .]
  I don't know him je ne le connais pas [. . . koh-nay
  pah]
  I don't know the area je ne connais pas la région
  do you know where/how? est-ce que vous savez
  où/comment? [esker voo sah-vay oo, koh-mōn]
label une étiquette [aytee-ket]
laces des lacets [lay-say]
lacquer de la lacque [lak]
lady: the lady here told me . . . cette dame m'a dit . . .
  [set dam mah dee]
  the ladies' les toilettes (des dames) [twah-let day
  dam]
lager une bière [bee-yair]
» *TRAVEL TIP: if you ask for 'une bière' you will
  automatically be served 'une bière blonde', which is
  lager-type beer (although it may taste different from
  what you are used to)*
lake un lac
lamb *(meat)* de l'agneau [ahn-yoh]
lamp une lampe [lōnp]

lampshade un abat-jour [ahbah-joor]
lamp-post un lampadaire [lonpah-dair]
land *(verb)* atterrir [ahtay-reer]
   (noun) la terre [tair]
   landscape le paysage [pay-ee-zahj]
lane une allée [ah-lay]
   (on motorway etc) une voie [vwah]
   the outside lane la voie de gauche [vwah der gohsh]
language une langue [long]
large grand [gron]
laryngitis une laryngite [lahran-jeet]
last dernier [dairn-yay]
   last year/week l'année/la semaine dernière
   last night hier soir [yair swahr]
   (during the night) la nuit dernière [lah nwee dairn-yair]
   at last! enfin! [onfan]
late tard [tahr]
   sorry I'm late je m'excuse, je suis en retard [jer mex-kooz jer swee on rer-tahr]
   later plus tard [ploo tahr]
   see you later à tout à l'heure [ah toot ah ler]
   at the latest au plus tard
laugh rire [reer]
launderette une laverie automatique [lahv-ree ohtoh-mah-teek]
lavabos toilets
lavatory les toilettes [twah-let]
lawyer un avocat [ahvoh-kah]
laxative un laxatif [laxah-teef]
lay-by une aire de stationnement [air der stahs-yohn-mon]
lazy paresseux [pahray-ser]
leader le chef [shef]
leaf une feuille [fer-ee]
leak une fuite [fweet]
   there's a leak in my ceiling il y a une fuite au plafond [. . . oh plah-fon]
   gas leak une fuite de gaz
   the petrol tank leaks le réservoir fuit [. . . fwee]
learn: I want to learn . . . je veux apprendre . . . [jer ver ah-prondr]
lease *(verb)* louer [lway]; *(noun)* le bail [bie]

least: not in the least pas du tout [pah doo too]
at least au moins [oh mwān]
the least le moins
leather du cuir [kweer]
leave *(go away)* partir [pahr-teer]
we're leaving tomorrow nous partons demain
[pahr-tōn . . .]
when does the bus leave? quand est-ce que le bus
part? [. . . pahr]
we left Paris yesterday nous avons quitté Paris hier
[nooz ah-vōn kee-tay . . .]
I left two shirts in my room j'ai laissé deux chemises
dans ma chambre [jay lay-say . . .]
can I leave this here/with you? est-ce que je peux
laisser ça ici/vous laisser ça? [esker jer per lay-say sah
ee-see, voo lay-say sah]
left: on the left à gauche [ah gohsh]
I'm left-handed je suis gaucher [jer swee goh-shay]
left-luggage (office) la consigne [kōn-seen]
leg la jambe [jōnb]
legal: is it legal? est-ce que c'est légal? [. . . lay-gal]
lemon un citron [see-trōn]
lemonade de la limonade [leemoh-nad]
lend: will you lend me . . .? est-ce que vous pouvez me
prêter . . .? [. . . pray-tay]
length la longueur [lōn-gherr]
lengthen rallonger [rahlōn-jay]
lens *(of camera)* l'objectif [l'objek-teef]
Lent le Carême [kah-raim]
less: less expensive/far (than) moins cher/loin (que)
[mwān . . . ker]
less milk/money moins de lait/d'argent
lesson: French/skiing lessons des leçons de
français/ski [ler-sōn . . .]
let *(flat etc)* louer [loo-ay]
let me help laissez-moi vous aider [lay-say mwah
vooz ay-day]
let me/him go laissez-moi/le partir
will you let me off here? laissez-moi descendre ici
[. . . day-sōndr ee-see]
let's go to allons à [ah-lōn ah]
let's go allons-y [ahlōnz-ee]
letter une lettre

are there any letters for me? est-ce qu'il y a du
courrier pour moi? [. . . doo koor-yay poor mwah]
letterbox une boîte aux lettres [bwaht oh laitr]
NB: start a letter with 'Monsieur' (or 'Madame',
'Mademoiselle') where you would have used 'Dear Sir'
etc, and with 'Cher Monsieur' etc where you would have
used 'Dear Mr Drew' etc. End the letter with 'Veuillez
agréer, Monsieur, l'expression de mes sentiments
distingués', or with 'Veuillez recevoir, cher Monsieur,
l'expression de mes meilleurs sentiments' (less formal)
lettuce une salade [sah-lad]
level: the oil level le niveau d'huile [nee-voh dweel]
  level-crossing un passage à niveau [pah-sahj ah
  nee-voh]
liable responsable [respōn-sahbl]
librairie bookshop
library une bibliothèque [beeblee-oh-tek]
libre vacant; free
libre-service self-service
licence un permis [pair-mee]
lid un couvercle [koo-vairkl]
lie un mensonge [mōn-sōnj]
  can he lie down for a bit? est-ce qu'il peut s'étendre
  un moment [eskeel per say-tōndr ān momōn]
life la vie [vee]
  life assurance une assurance-vie [ahsoo-rōns-vee]
  lifebelt la bouée de sauvetage
  [boo-ay der sohv-tahj]
  lifeboat le canot de sauvetage [kah-noh . . .]
  life-guard le surveillant de plage
  [soorvay-yān der plahj]
  life-jacket le gilet de sauvetage [jee-lay . . .]
lift: do you want a lift? est-ce que je peux vous
  emmener quelque part? [. . . vooz ōnm-nay kel-ker
  pahr]
  could you give me a lift (to Paris)? est-ce que vous
  pouvez m'emmener (jusqu'à Paris)? [. . . joos-kah . . .]
  the lift isn't working l'ascenseur ne marche pas
  [lahsōn-serr ner marsh pah]
light *(not heavy)* léger [lay-jay]
  (not dark) clair [klair]
  the lights aren't working *(house)* la lumière ne
  s'allume pas [lah loom-yair ner sah-loom pah]

(car) les phares ne s'allument pas [lay fahr . . .]
have you got a light? est-ce que vous avez du feu?
[esker vooz ah-vay doo fer]
can you put the light on/turn the light off? est-ce
que vous pouvez allumer/éteindre [ay-tāndr] la
lumière?
when it gets light quand il fait jour [kōnt eel fay joor]
light bulb une ampoule [ōn-pool]
light meter le posemètre [pohz-maitr]
lighter un briquet [bree-kay]
like *(the same as)* comme [kom]
would you like . . . ? est-ce que vous voulez . . . ?
[esker voo voo-lay]
I'd like a coffee *etc* j'aimerais un café *etc*
[jaym-ray . . .]
I'd like to go j'aimerais partir
I like it ça me plaît [sah mer play]
I like you vous me plaisez [voo mer play-zay]
I don't like it ça ne me plaît pas
he doesn't like it ça ne lui plaît pas [. . . lwee play
pah]
what's it like? c'est comment? [say koh-mōn]
do it like this faites comme ça [fayt kom sah]
one like that un comme ça [ān kom sah]
lime un citron vert [see-trōn vair]
line la ligne [leen]
lip la lèvre [laivr]
lipstick du rouge à lèvres [rooj ah laivr]
lip salve de la pommade [poh-mad] pour les lèvres
liqueur une liqueur [lee-kerr]
list une liste [leest]
price list le tarif [tah-reef]
listen écouter [aykoo-tay]
litre un litre [leetr]
» *TRAVEL TIP: 1 litre = 1¾ pints = 0.22 gals*
pints 0.44 0.87 1.75 3.50 5.25
litres 0.25 0.5 1 2 3
little *(small)* petit [per-tee]
a little un peu [ān per]
a little ice un peu de glace
a little more un peu plus [. . . ploo]
live¹: I live in London/England j'habite à Londres/en
Angleterre [jah-beet ah lōndr, ōnn ōngler-tair]

....

where do you live? où est-ce que vous habitez? [wesker vooz ahbee-tay]

live² *(TV)* en direct [on dee-rekt]
  (wire etc) sous tension [soo tons-yon]
liver le foie [fwah]
  liver pate du pâté de foie
loaf un pain [pan]
lobster une langouste [lon-goost]
local: a local wine un vin de la région [. . . der lah rayj-yon]
  a local restaurant un restaurant du coin [. . . doo kwan]
  is it made locally? est-ce que c'est fait ici? [esker say fay ee-see]
location de voitures car hire
lock: the lock's broken la serrure est abîmée [lah say-roor ayt ahbee-may]
  it's locked c'est fermé à clé [fair-may ah klay]
  I've locked myself out/in je me suis enfermé dehors/dedans [jer mer swee onfair-may der-ohr, der-don]
  locker un casier [kahz-yay] (qui ferme à clé)
London Londres [londr]
lonely: I feel lonely je me sens seul [jer mer son serl]
long long [lon]
  will it take long? est-ce que ça va prendre longtemps? [. . . sah vah prondr lon-ton]
  we'd like to stay longer nous aimerions rester plus longtemps [nooz aymer-yon res-tay ploo lon-ton]
  that was long ago c'était il y a longtemps [say-tay eel-yah . . .]
loo: where's the loo? où sont les toilettes? [oo son lay twah-let]
look: he looks ill/tired il a l'air malade/fatigué [eel ah lair . . .]
  it looks unsafe ça a l'air dangereux [sah ah lair . . .]
  it looks nice c'est joli [say . . .]
  look at that regardez ça [rergahr-day sah]
  can I look? est-ce que je peux regarder?
  I'm just looking je regarde [jer rer-gahrd]
  I'm looking forward to . . . je me réjouis de . . . [jer mer ray-jwee der]
  I'm looking for . . . je cherche . . . [jer shairsh]

look out! attention! [ahtōns-yōn]
loose *(undone)* défait [day-fay]
lorry un camion [kahm-yōn]
    lorry driver un chauffeur de camion
    [shoh-ferr . . .]
lose perdre [pairdr]
    I've lost my . . . j'ai perdu mon (ma) . . .
    [jay pair-doo . . .]
    I'm lost je me suis perdu [jer mer swee pair-doo]
    lost property office le bureau des objets trouvés
    [boo-roh dayz ob-jay troo-vay]
lot: a lot (of) beaucoup (de) [boh-koo der]
    not a lot pas beaucoup
    a lot more expensive (than) beaucoup plus cher
    (que) [. . . ploo shair ker]
lotion une lotion [lohs-yōn]
loud fort [fohr]
    speak louder parlez plus fort [pahr-lay ploo fohr]
à *louer* *to let*
lounge le salon [sah-lōn]
    departure lounge la salle d'embarquement [sahl
    dōnbar-ker-mōn]
love: I love you je vous aime [jer vooz aim]
    he's in love (with) il est amoureux (de) [eel ayt
    ahmoo-rer]
    I love this wine j'aime beaucoup ce vin
    [jaim boh-koo . . .]
lovely *(view etc)* très joli [tray joh-lee]
    (dish etc) délicieux [daylees-yer]
    we had a lovely holiday nous avons passé de
    merveilleuses vacances [nooz ah-vōn pah-say der
    mairvay-yerz vah-kōns]
low bas [bah]
luck: good luck! bonne chance! [bon shōns]
    you're lucky vous avez de la chance [vooz ah-vay der
    lah shōns]
    that's lucky c'est de la chance
luggage les bagages [bah-gahj]
    luggage rack le porte-bagages
    [port-bah-gahj]
lumbago un lumbago [lānbah-goh]
lump *(on body)* une grosseur [groh-serr]
    (of sugar) un morceau [mohr-soh]

....

lunch le déjeuner [day-jer-nay]
YOU MAY SEE OR HEAR . . .
plat du jour [plah doo jour] *set menu*
» *TRAVEL TIP: the set menu is generally well worth
trying; in Switzerland, 'déjeuner' is commonly used for
'breakfast'; use 'dîner' for lunch*
lungs les poumons [poo-mōn]
luxurious luxueux [looxoo-er]
luxury: a luxury hotel un hôtel de luxe [. . . der loox]
mad fou (folle) [foo, fol]
machine une machine [mah-sheen]
Madam Madame [mah-dam]
made-to-measure fait sur mesure [fay soor mer-zoor]
magazine un magazine [mahgah-zeen]
magnificent magnifique [mahnee-feek]
maiden name le nom de jeune fille [nōn der jern fee]
mail: can you mail this for me? est-ce que vous
pouvez me poster ça? [. . . mer pos-tay sah]
is there any mail for me? est-ce qu'il y a du courrier
pour moi? [eskeel-yah doo koor-yay poor mwah]
main principal [prānsee-pal]
the main roads les grandes routes [grōnd root]
make faire [fair]
will we make it in time? est-ce qu'on y arrivera à
temps? [eskōnn ee ahreev-rah ah tōn]
who is it made by? c'est fabriqué par qui? [say
fahbree-kay par kee]
make-up le maquillage [mahkee-yahj]
man un homme [om]
the man at the desk said . . . le monsieur au guichet
m'a dit . . . [ler mers-yer . . .]
manager: I would like to see the manager j'aimerais
parler au directeur [jem-ray par-lay oh deerek-terr]
manageress la directrice [deerek-trees]
manicure: can I have a manicure? est-ce qu'on peut
me faire les mains? [eskōn per mer fair lay mān]
many beaucoup [boh-koo]
many places/people beaucoup d'endroits/de gens
map une carte [kart]
a local map une carte de la région [. . . der la
rayj-yōn]
road map une carte routière [. . . root-yair]
a map of Paris un plan de Paris [ān plōn der pah-ree]

March: in March en mars [mahrs]
margarine de la margarine [mahrgah-reen]
marina un port de plaisance [pohr der play-zōns]
mark une marque [mahrk]
market un marché [mahr-shay]
  when is market day? quand est-ce que c'est jour de
  marché? [kōnt esker say joor der mahr-shay]
marmalade de la confiture d'oranges [kōnfee-toor
  doh-rōnj]
married marié [mahr-yay]
marry: we were married in 1960 nous nous sommes
  mariés en 1960 [noo noo som mahr-yay ōn . . .]
  will you marry me? voulez-vous m'épouser?
  [voolay-voo maypoo-zay]
marvellous merveilleux [mairvay-yer]
mascara du mascara
mashed potatoes de la purée de pommes de terre
  [poo-ray der pom der tair]
mass *(in church)* la messe [mess]
massage un massage [mah-sahj]
mast mât [mah]
mat un petit tapis [per-tee tah-pee]
match: a box of matches une boîte d'allumettes
  [bwaht dahloo-met]
  football match un match de football
material *(cloth)* du tissu [tee-soo]
matter: it doesn't matter ça ne fait rien [sah ner fay
  ree-yān]
  what's the matter? qu'est-ce qui ne va pas? [keskee
  ner vah pah]
mattress un matelas [mat-lah]
mature mûr [moor]
maximum le maximum [maxee-mom]
may: may I have/take . . . ? est-ce que je peux avoir/
  prendre . . .? [esker jer per ah-vwahr, prōndr]
  may we . . .? est-ce que nous pouvons . . .? [esker noo
  poo-vōn]
May: in May en mai [may]
maybe peut-être [pert-aitr]
mayonnaise de la mayonnaise [mah-yoh-nayz]
me: he knows me il me [mer] connaît
  he saw me il m'a vu
  give me . . . donnez-moi . . . [. . . mwah]

give it to me donnez-le moi
it's me c'est moi [say mwah]
meal un repas [rer-pah]
mean: what does this mean? qu'est-ce que ça veut
dire? [kesker sah ver deer]
by all means! bien entendu! [bee-yann onton-doo]
measles la rougeole [roo-johl]
German measles la rubéole [roobay-ohl]
measure mesurer [merzoo-ray]
measurements les dimensions [deemons-yon]
meat de la viande [vee-yond]
mechanic: is there a mechanic here? est-ce qu'il y a
un mécanicien ici? [eskeel-yah an maykah-nees-yan
ee-see]
medical: medical treatment un traitement
[trait-mon]
medicine (drug) un remède [rer-maid]
meet rencontrer
I met him last year je l'ai rencontré l'année dernière
[jer lay ronkon-tray . . .]
when shall we meet? quand est-ce que nous nous
voyons? [kontes-ker noo noo vwah-yon]
pleased to meet you enchanté(e) de faire votre
connaissance [onshon-tay der fair vohtr kohnay-sons]
meeting une réunion [ray-oon-yon]
melon un melon [mer-lon]
member un membre [monmbr]
how do I become a member? comment est-ce que je
peux devenir membre? [koh-mont esker jer per
derver-neer . . .]
memories les souvenirs
mend: can you mend this? est-ce que vous pouvez
réparer ça? [. . . raypah-ray sah]
mention: don't mention it je vous en prie [jer vooz on
pree]
menu: can I see the menu, please? est-ce que je peux
voir la carte, s'il vous plaît? [esker jer per vwahr lah
kart . . .]
we'll have the set menu nous prenons le plat du jour
[noo prer-non ler plah doo joor]
do you have a set-price menu? est-ce que vous avez
un menu touristique? [. . . mer-noo toorees-teek]

» TRAVEL TIP: see the menu reader pp. 72–73

mess: my room is in a mess ma chambre est en
désordre [. . . ōn day-zohrdr]
message: are there any messages for me?
est-ce qu'il y a une commission pour moi? [eskeel-yah
oon kohmees-yōn poor mwah]
can I leave a message for . . .? est-ce que je peux
laisser un mot pour . . .? [. . . lay-say ān moh poor]
messieurs men
metre un mètre [maitr]
» *TRAVEL TIP: 1 metre = 39.37 ins = 1.09 yds*

feet	3.3	6.6	10	16.6	33	333
metres	1	2	3	5	10	100

meter un compteur [kōn-terr]
has the meter been read? est-ce qu'on a relevé le
compteur? [eskōnn ah rerl-vay . . .]
métro underground
» *TRAVEL TIP: flat fare on whole network of Paris métro;*
a 'carnet de tickets' (book of 10 tickets) is more
economical than single tickets; tickets valid on Paris
bus network, but not on 'RER' (Greater Paris fast
commuter train)
midday midi [mee-dee]
at midday à midi
middle le milieu [meel-yer]
in the middle (of) au milieu (de)
midnight minuit [meen-wee]
at midnight à minuit
might: I might be late je serai peut-être en retard [jer
ser-ray pert-aitr . . .]
I might come je viendrai peut-être [jer vee-yān-dray
pert-aitr]
he might have gone il est peut-être parti [eel ay
pert-aitr . . .]
migraine une migraine [mee-grain]
mild doux [doo]
mile un mille [meel]
» *TRAVEL TIP: conversion: miles ÷ 5 × 8 = kilometres*

miles	0.5	1	3	5	10	50	100
kilometres	0.8	1.6	4.8	8	16	80	160

milk du lait [lay]
a glass of milk un verre de lait [vair der lay]
milkshake un milkshake
millimetre un millimètre [meelee-maitr]

Entrées: Starters
Crudités *various salads and raw vegetables*
Terrine du chef *pâté maison*
Oeufs mayonnaise *egg mayonnaise*
Bouchées à la reine *chicken vol-au-vent*

Potages: Soups
Crème de bolets *cream of mushroom*
Velouté de tomates *cream of tomato*
Soupe à l'oignon *onion soup*

Viandes: Meat dishes
Boeuf *beef*, porc *pork*, veau *veal*, agneau *lamb*
Rôti de boeuf *roast beef*
Gigot d'agneau *roast leg of lamb*
Côtelette de porc *pork chop*
Foie de veau *veal liver*
Langue de boeuf *tongue*
Bifteck *steak*
Tournedos *fillet steak*
Escalope panée *slice of veal in breadcrumbs*
Paupiettes de veau *veal olives*
Rognons madère *kidneys in madeira sauce*

Volaille: poultry
Poule au riz *chicken and rice*
Poulet rôti *roast chicken*
Canard à l'orange *duck with orange*

Chasse: game
Civet de lièvre *jugged hare*
Lapin chasseur *rabbit in white wine and herbs*

Poissons et marée: fish and seafood
Coquilles Saint-Jacques *scallops*
Huîtres *oysters*
Moules marinière *mussels in white wine*
Truite aux amandes *trout with almonds*
Raie au beurre noir *skate in black butter*
Homard à l'armoricaine *lobster in white wine sauce with shallots*
Cabillaud *cod*, langouste *crayfish*, langoustine *scampi*, morue *salt cod*

A few menu terms: à l'ail *(with) garlic*, aux câpres *in caper sauce*, à la crème *with cream*, garni *with chips (or rice) and vegetables*, en gelée *in aspic*, provençale *cooked in olive oil with garlic, tomatoes and herbs*, au vin blanc *in white wine*, vinaigrette *sharp vinegar dressing*

Légumes: vegetables
Pommes de terre à l'anglaise *steamed potatoes*, pommes dauphine *potato croquettes*, (pommes) frites *chips*, purée *mashed potatoes*

Chou *cabbage*, chou-fleur *cauliflower*, courgettes *baby marrows*, épinards *spinach*, haricots verts *French beans*, petits pois *peas*

Salads
Salade *green salad with French dressing*
Salade niçoise *with green beans, peppers, anchovies, olives*
Salade russe *mixed vegetable in mayonnaise*

Fromages: le plateau de fromages *cheese board*

Dessert
Glace *ice-cream*, flan *egg custard*
Tarte aux myrtilles *bilberry tart*
Cerises *cherries*, fraises *strawberries*, poire *pear*, pomme *apple*, pêche *peach*, raisin *grapes*

Snacks
Assiette anglaise *cold meats*, saucisse, frites *Frankfurter sausage and chips*, crêpes *pancakes*, croque-monsieur *toasted ham and cheese sandwich*, omelette au jambon/fromage *ham/cheese omelette*, sandwich aux rillettes *potted meat sandwich*

Wines: *apart from the well-known 'beaujolais' or more expensive 'bourgogne' and 'bordeaux', try 'Côtes du Rhône' (red or white) and Anjou wines (rosé or white)*
sec *dry*, demi-sec *medium dry*

Enjoy your meal! – or, as they say, **bon appétit!**

milometer = le compteur kilométrique [kōn-terr keeloh-may-treek]
minced meat de la viande hachée [vee-yōnd ah-shay]
mind: I've changed my mind j'ai changé d'avis [jay shōn-jay dah-vee]
   I don't mind ça ne me dérange pas [sahn mer day-rōnj pah]
   (it's all the same) ça m'est égal [sah mayt ay-gal]
   do you mind if I ...? est-ce que ça vous dérange si ...? [esker sah voo day-rōnj see]
   never mind tant pis [tōn pee]
mine *see* **my**
mineral water de l'eau minérale [oh meenay-rahl]
minimum le minimum [meenee-mom]
   the minimum charge le tarif minimum
minus moins [mwān]
minute une minute [mee-noot]
   in a minute dans un instant [dōnz ān āns-tōn]
   just a minute un instant
mirror une glace [glahs]
   (rear view) le rétroviseur [raytroh-vee-zerr]
Miss Mademoiselle [mahd-mwah-zel]
miss: we missed the train/boat nous avons manqué le train/bateau [nooz ah-vōn mōn-kay ...]
   I miss you vous me manquez [voo mer mōn-kay]
   my wallet/sister is missing mon portefeuille/ma soeur a disparu [... ah deespah-roo]
   there's something/there are 2 people missing il y a quelque chose qui manque/deux personnes qui manquent [eelyah kelker-shohz ... kee mōnk]
mist la brume [broom]
mistake une erreur [ay-rerr]
   I think you've made a mistake je crois que vous vous êtes trompé [jer krwah ker voo vooz ait trōn-pay]
misunderstanding: there's been a misunderstanding il y a eu un malentendu [eelyah oo ān mahlōn-tōn-doo]
mix mélanger [maylōn-jay]
modern moderne [moh-dairn]
moisturizer une lotion hydratante [lohs-yōn eedrah-tōnt]
moment un moment [moh-mōn]
Monday lundi [lān-dee]

money: I've lost my money j'ai perdu mon argent [jay pair-doo mōn ahr-jōn]
I have no money je n'ai pas d'argent [jer nay pah dahr-jōn]
» *TRAVEL TIP: French currency*
The unit is 'un franc', divided up into 100 'centimes'; main coins are 10 centimes, 20c, 50c, 1F, 2F, 5F and 10F; the 10F coin is easily mistaken for other large coins; main notes are 10F, 20F, 50F, 100F, 500F
month un mois [mwah]
monument un monument [mohnoo-mōn]
moon la lune [loon]
moorings *(ropes)* les amarres [ah-mahr]
moped un cyclomoteur [seekloh-moh-terr]
more plus [ploo(s)]
    more expensive (than) plus cher (que) [ploo shair ker]
    more people/money plus de gens/d'argent [ploos der . . .]
    can I have some more? est-ce que je peux en avoir plus? [. . . ōnn ah-vwahr ploos]
    more wine, please encore du vin, s'il vous plaît [ōn-kor doo vān . . .]
    no more, thank you merci, ça suffit [mair-see sah soo-fee]
    no more money plus [ploo] d'argent
    I haven't got any more je n'en ai plus [jer nōnn ay ploo]
    there aren't any more il n'y en a plus [eeln yōnn ah ploo]
morning le matin [mah-tān]
    in the morning le matin
    the following morning le lendemain matin [lōnd-mān mah-tān]
mosquito un moustique [moos-teek]
most: the most . . . le plus . . . [ler ploo]
    I like this one the most c'est celui-ci que je préfère [say ser-lwee-see ker jer pray-fair]
    most of the time/the people la plupart du temps/des gens [lah ploo-par doo tōn, day jōn]
    that's most kind c'est très gentil [say tray jōn-tee]
motel un motel [moh-tel]
mother: my mother ma mère [mair]

motor le moteur [moh-ter]
motorbike une moto [moh-toh]
motorboat un canot automobile [kah-noh ohtoh-moh-beel]
motorcyclist un motocycliste [mohtoh-see-kleest]
motorist un automobiliste [ohtoh-moh-bee-leest]
motorway l'autoroute [ohtoh-root]
» *TRAVEL TIP: toll motorways in France (relatively expensive); you either pay at the 'péage' (toll-station) or get a card there and pay on exit; most M-ways are 2-lane only: be extra careful where lanes merge; the Paris ring road ('le périphérique') is toll-free*
mountain une montagne [mōn-tan]
   in the mountains à la montagne
   mountaineering l'alpinisme [alpee-neesm]
mouse une souris [soo-ree]
moustache une moustache [moos-tahsh]
mouth la bouche [boosh]
move bouger [boo-jay]
   don't move ne bougez pas [ner boo-jay pah]
   could you move your car? est-ce que vous pouvez déplacer votre voiture? [. . . dayplah-say vohtr vwah-toor]
Mrs Madame [mah-dam], Mme
Ms *no equivalent in French*
much beaucoup [boh-koo]
   much better/much more beaucoup mieux/plus
   not much pas beaucoup [pah . . .]
mug: I've been mugged j'ai été attaqué [ahtah-kay]
   coffee mug une grande tasse [grōnd tahs]
muscle un muscle [mooskl]
   I've strained a muscle je me suis claqué un muscle [jer mer swee klah-kay . . .]
museum un musée [moo-zay]
» *TRAVEL TIP: most museums and castles are closed on Tuesdays in France*
mushroom un champignon [shōnpeen-yōn]
music la musique [moo-zeek]
mussels des moules [mool]
must devoir [der-vwahr]
   I must go je dois partir [jer dwah . . .]
   we must not . . . nous ne devons pas . . . [noo ner der-vōn pah]

you must... vous devez ... [voo der-vay]
mustard de la moutarde
mutton du mouton [moo-tōn]
my mon [mōn], ma [mah], *(plural)* mes [may]
  it's my bag, it's mine c'est mon sac, c'est le mien
  [... ler mee-yān]
  it's my car, it's mine c'est ma voiture, c'est la mienne
  [... lah mee-yen] *(plural:* 'les miens, les miennes')
nail *(on finger)* un ongle [ōngl]
  (in wood etc) un clou [kloo]
  nail clippers une pince à ongles [pāns ...]
  nail file une lime à ongles [leem ...]
  nail polish du vernis à ongles [vair-nee ...]
  nail scissors des ciseaux à ongles [see-zoh ...]
naked nu [noo]
name un nom [nōn]
  my name is... je m'appelle ... [jer mah-pel]
  what's your name? quel est votre nom? [kel-ay vohtr
  nōn]
  what's the name of...? comment s'appelle ...?
  [koh-mōn sah-pel]
napkin une serviette [sairv-yet]
nappies les couches [koosh]
  disposable nappies des couches à jeter [... ah
  jer-tay]
  nappy liners les protège-couches [proh-tayj-koosh]
narrow étroit [ay-trwah]
national national [nahs-yoh-nal]
nationality la nationalité [nahs-yoh-nah-
lee-tay]
natural naturel [nahtoo-rel]
naughty: don't be naughty soyez sage [swah-yay
sahj]
near: is it near? est-ce que c'est près? [esker say pray]
  near here/home près d'ici/de chez nous [pray
  dee-see, der shay noo]
  where's the nearest chemist/bank? où est la
  pharmacie/banque la plus proche? [oo ay ... lah ploo
  prosh]
  do you go near...? est-ce que vous passez près
  de ...? [... pah-say pray der]
  nearly presque [presk]
neat *(drink)* sec

....

necessary nécessaire [naysay-sair]
neck le cou [koo]
necklace le collier [kol-yay]
need: I need a ... j'ai besoin d'un ... [jay ber-zwan]
  he needs ... il a besoin de ...
  I/we need to leave je dois/nous devons partir [jer dwah, noo der-von ...]
needle une aiguille [ay-gwee]
negative *(photo)* un négatif [naygah-teef]
neighbour un voisin [vwah-zan]
neither: neither of them aucun des deux [oh-kan day der]
  neither I nor ... ni moi ni ... [nee mwah nee]
  neither do I moi non plus [mwah non ploo]
nephew: my nephew mon neveu [ner-ver]
nervous nerveux [nair-ver]
net: net price le prix net [pree net]
nettoyage à sec dry cleaning
never jamais [jah-may]
  I've never been there je n'y suis jamais allé [jer nee swee jah-may ah-lay]
new nouveau [noo-voh]
  (not used) neuf [nerf]
news les nouvelles [noo-vel]
  newsagent un kiosque à journaux [kee-yosk ah joor-noh]
  newspaper un journal [joor-nal]
  do you have any English newspapers?
  est-ce que vous avez des journaux anglais? [... day joor-noh on-glay]
New Year la nouvelle année [noo-vel ah-nay]
  on New Year's day le jour de l'An [ler joor der lon]
» *TRAVEL TIP: usually an occasion for a big meal with friends, 'le réveillon'* [rayvay-yon]
  on New Year's Eve à la Saint Sylvestre [ah lah san seel-vaistr]
  happy New Year bonne année [bon ah-nay]
New Zealand la Nouvelle Zélande [noo-vel zay-lond]
next *(bus, train)* prochain [pro-shan]
  next to ... à côté de ... [ah koh-tay der]
  stop at the next corner arrêtez-vous au prochain croisement
  [ahray-tay voo oh proh-shan krwahz-mon]

see you next year! à l'année prochaine! [ah lay-nay proh-shān]

next week la semaine prochaine [lah ser-main proh-shān]

when is the next train? quand part le prochain train? [kōn par ler proh-shān. . .]

where is the next stop? où est le prochain arrêt? [oo ay ler proh-shain ah-ray]

nice *(nice-looking)* joli [joh-lee]

   (pleasant, kind) gentil [jōn-tee]

niece: my niece ma nièce [nee-yes]

night la nuit [nwee]

   at night la nuit

   night club un night-club

   night-dress une chemise de nuit [sher-meez . . .]

   night porter le portier de nuit [pohrt-yay . . .]

no *(reply)* non [nōn]

   there's no water/toilet paper il n'y a pas d'eau/de papier hygiénique [eelnyah pah der . . .]

   I've no money je n'ai pas d'argent [jer nay pah . . .]

nobody personne [pair-son]

   nobody saw him personne ne l'a vu [pair-son ner . . .]

noise le bruit [brwee]

   it's very noisy il y a beaucoup de bruit

   our room is too noisy notre chambre est trop bruyante [nohtr shōnbr ay troh brwee-yōnt]

none aucun [oh-kān]

   none of them aucun d'entre eux [. . . dōntr er]

nonsense: I don't want any nonsense je ne veux pas d'histoires [jern ver pah dees-twahr]

non-smoker non-fumeurs [nōn foo-mer]

noon: at noon à midi [mee-dee]

normal normal [nohr-mal]

north le nord [nor]

North America l'Amérique du Nord [ahmay-reek doo nor]

Northern Ireland l'Irlande du Nord [eer-lōnd doo nor]

nose le nez [nay]

   I have a nosebleed je saigne du nez [jer sayn . . .]

not pas [pah]

   not me/that one pas moi/celui-là

   I'm not hungry je n'ai pas faim [jer nay pah . . .]

he's not here il n'est pas là [eel nay pah . . .]
I don't want . . . je ne veux pas . . . [jer ner ver pah]
he doesn't understand il ne comprend pas [eel
ner . . . pah]
I didn't . . . je n'ai pas . . .
he didn't tell me il ne m'a pas dit
there isn't any . . . il n'y a pas de . . .
note *(bank note)* un billet (de banque) [bee-yay der
bonk]
notepaper du papier à lettres [pahp-yay ah laitr]
nothing rien [ree-yān]
  there's nothing il n'y a rien
notice: I didn't notice (that) . . . je n'ai pas remarqué
(que) . . . [jer nay pah rermahr-kay ker]
November: in November en novembre [noh-vōnbr]
now maintenant [mānt-nōn]
nowhere nulle part [nool par]
nudist un nudiste [noo-deest]
  nudist beach une plage réservée aux nudistes
nuisance: it's a nuisance c'est ennuyeux
[sayt ōn-nwee-yer]
  he's being a nuisance il nous importune [eel nooz
ānpor-toon]
numb engourdi [ōngoor-dee]
number le numéro [noomay-roh]
  (quantity) le nombre [nōnbr]
  number plates les plaques d'immatriculation [plak
deemah-tree-koo-lahs-yōn]
nurse une infirmière [ānfeerm-yair]
nursery slope une piste pour débutants [peest poor
dayboo-tōn]
nut *(for bolt)* un écrou [ay-kroo]
  (to eat) no single general term: be specific
  see **peanuts**
nylon du nylon [nee-lon]
oar une rame [rahm]
objets trouvés lost property
obligatory obligatoire [ohblee-gah-twahr]
obvious: it's obvious c'est évident [set ayvee-dōn]
occasionally de temps en temps [der tōnz ōn tōn]
occupied: is this seat occupied? est-ce que cette
place est prise? [. . . set plass ay preez]
o'clock *see* **time**

October: in October en octobre [oōn ok-tohbr]
octopus un poulpe [poolp]
odd *(strange)* bizarre
    odd number un nombre impair [noōnbr aān-pair]
off: the milk is off le lait a tourné [. . . ah toor-nay]
    this meat is off cette viande n'est plus bonne
    [. . . ploo boōn]
    10% off dix pour cent de réduction [dee poor soōn der
    raydooks-yoōn]
    it came off c'est tombé [say toōn-bay]
    can you switch it off? est-ce que vous pouvez
    l'éteindre? [. . . ay-taāndr]
offence un délit [day-lee]
offensive injurieux [aānjoor-yer]
offer: can I offer you . . .? puis-je vous offrir . . .?
    [pweej vooz oh-freer]
office un bureau [boo-roh]
officer *(to policeman)* Monsieur l'agent [mers-yer
    lah-joōn]
official officiel [ohfees-yel]
    (person) un employé [oōnplwah-yay]
often souvent [soo-voōn]
oil de l'huile [weel]
    (cooking) de l'huile comestible [kohmes-teebl]
    (petroleum) du pétrole [pay-trol]
    I'm losing oil je perds [pair] de l'huile
    will you change the oil? est-ce que vous pouvez me
    faire une vidange? [. . . mer fair oon vee-doōnj]
ointment une pommade [poh-mad]
O.K. d'accord [dah-kor]
    it's O.K. ça va [sah vah]
old vieux (vieille) [vee-yer, vee-yay]
    how old are you? quel âge avez-vous? [kel ahj ah-vay
    voo]
olive une olive [oh-leev]
    green/black olives des olives vertes/noires
    [. . . vairt, nwahr]
omelette une omelette
    cheese/ham omelette une omelette au
    fromage/jambon [ohm-let oh froh-mahj, joōn-boōn]
on sur [soor]
    I haven't got it on me je ne l'ai pas sur moi [jer ner
    lay pah soor mwah]

put the light on allumez la lumière [ahloo-may . . .]
on Monday etc lundi etc
on Mondays etc le lundi etc
on television à la télévision
once une fois [oon fwah]
  at once tout de suite [toot sweet]
one un (une) [ān, oon]
  the red one le (la) rouge
  one way street une rue à sens unique [roo ah sōns oo-neek]
onion un oignon [ohn-yōn]
only seulement [serl-mōn]
open ouvert [oo-vair]
  when do you open? quand est-ce que vous ouvrez? [kōnt esker vooz oo-vray]
  I can't open it je n'arrive pas à l'ouvrir [jer nah-reev pah ah loo-vreer]
  open return un billet de retour 'open' [bee-yay der rer-toor . . .]
opera un opéra [ohpay-rah]
  opera house l'opéra
operation une opération [ohpay-rahs-yōn]
  will I need an operation? est-ce qu'il faudra m'opérer? [eskeel foh-drah mohpay-ray]
operator *(telephone)* l'opératrice [ohpay-rah-trees]
» *TRAVEL TIP: dial 10 to call the operator, and 12 ('renseignements') for international calls and enquiries*
opposite en face (de) [ōn fahs der]
optician un opticien [optees-yān]
or ou [oo]
orange une orange [oh-rōnj]
  orange juice un jus [joo] d'orange
orchestra un orchestre [ohr-kestr]
order: could we order now? est-ce qu'on peut commander maintenant? [eskōn per kohmōn-day mānt-nōn]
  thank you, we've already ordered merci, nous avons déjà commandé
  it's out of order ça ne marche pas [sah ner marsh pah]
original original [ohree-jee-nal]
other autre [ohtr]

the other one l'autre
do you have any others? est-ce que vous en avez
d'autres?
otherwise autrement [ohtrer-mon]
ought: I ought to go je devrais partir [jer der-vray
par-teer]
ounce 1 ounce = 28.35 grammes
our notre [nohtr], nos [noh]
our car/son notre voiture/fils
our tickets/cars nos billets/voitures
it's ours c'est le (la) nôtre [ler, lah nohtr]
these are ours ce sont les nôtres [lay nohtr]
out dehors [der-ohr]
we're out of petrol nous n'avons plus d'essence [noo
nah-von ploo . . .]
outboard un hors-bord [ohr-bohr]
outdoors dehors [der-ohr]
outside dehors [der-ohr]
can we sit outside? est-ce qu'on peut se mettre
dehors?
ouvert open
over: over here ici [ee-see]
over there là-bas [lah-bah]
he's over 40 il a plus de [ploo der] quarante ans
it's all over c'est fini [say fee-nee]
overboard: man overboard! un homme à la mer!
[ann om ah lah mair]
overcharge: you've overcharged me la facture est
trop élevée [lah fak-toor ay trohp ayl-vay]
overcooked trop cuit [troh kwee]
overexposed surexposé [soorex-poh-zay]
overnight la nuit [nwee]
we want to stay overnight nous voulons passer la
nuit ici [. . . pah-say la nwee . . .]
oversleep: I overslept j'ai dormi trop longtemps [jay
dor-mee troh lon-ton]
overtake dépasser [daypah-say]
owe: what do I/we owe you? combien est-ce que je
vous dois/nous vous devons? [konb-yan esker jer voo
dwah, noo voo der-von]
you owe me 10F vous me devez dix francs [voo mer
der-vay]
own: my own . . . mon propre . . . [prohpr]

I'm on my own je suis seul [jer swee serl]

owner le propriétaire [prohpree-yay-tair]

oxygen l'oxygène [oxee-jen]

oysters des huîtres [weetr]

pack: I haven't packed yet je n'ai pas encore fait mes bagages
[jer nay pahz on-kot fay may bah-gahj]
can I have a packed lunch? est-ce que je peux avoir un pique-nique? [. . . peek-neek]
package tour un voyage organisé [voh-yahj orgah-nee-zay]

packet: a packet of . . . un paquet de . . . [pah-kay]

padlock un verrou [vay-roo]

page la page [pahj]
could you page him? est-ce que vous pouvez le faire appeler? [. . . ler fair ap-lay]

pain: I've got a pain here j'ai mal ici [jay mal ce-see]
I've got a pain in my leg/back j'ai mal à la jambe/aux reins
painkillers des calmants [kal-mon]

painful douloureux [dooloo-rer]

painting un tableau [tah-bloh]

pair: pair of gloves/shoes une paire de gants/chaussures [pair der . . .]

pale pâle [pahl]

pancake une crêpe [kraip]

panties un slip

pants (*underpants*) un slip
(*trousers*) un pantalon [pontah-lon]

paper (*newspaper*) un journal [joor-nal]
a piece of paper un (morceau de) papier [mohr-soh der pahp-yay]
paper hankies des mouchoirs en papier [moo-shwahr . . .]

paraffin *paraffin oil is not used in France for domestic purposes*

parcel un colis [koh-lee]

pardon (*I didn't understand*) pardon . . . [pahr-don]
I beg your pardon (*sorry*) excusez-moi [exkoo-zay mwah]

parents: my parents mes parents [pah-ron]

Paris Paris [pah-ree]

park *(noun)* un parc
  where can I park my car? où est-ce que je peux garer ma voiture? [wesker jer per gah-ray mah vwah-toor]
» *TRAVEL TIP: disc zones in most towns: you must display a 'disque de stationnement' (parking disc) on your windscreen; for further information go to the local 'syndicat d'initiative' (tourist office)*
part: part of une partie de [pahr-tee der]
  (spare) part une pièce de rechange [pee-yes der rer-shōnj]
partner *(business)* un associé [ahsohs-yay]
  (games) un partenaire [parter-nair]
party *(group)* un groupe [groop]
  (celebration) une réunion [ray-oon-yōn]
  (in the evening) une soirée [swah-ray]
  I'm with the English party je suis avec le groupe anglais
pass *(mountain)* un col
  he's passed out il s'est évanoui [eel sayt ayvah-nwee]
passable *(road)* praticable [prah-tee-kahbl]
passage souterrain subway
  passage protégé stretch of main road where traffic coming from the side roads doesn't have right of way
passenger un passager [pahsah-jay]
passer-by un passant [pah-sōn]
passport: my passport mon passeport [pass-pohr]
past: in the past autrefois [ohtr-fwah]
  do you go past the station? est-ce que vous passez devant la gare? [esker voo pah-say der-vōn . . .]
pasta des pâtes [paht]
pastry de la pâtisserie [pahtees-ree]
path un chemin [sher-mān]
patient: be patient soyez patient [swah-yay pahs-yōn]
pâtisserie baker's
pattern *(design)* un dessin [day-sān]
pavement le trottoir [troh-twahr]
pay *(verb)* payer [pay-yay]
  can I pay, please? est-ce que je peux payer, s'il vous plaît?
PCV: communication en PCV reverse charge call
pea: peas des petits pois [per-tee pwah]

peace la paix [pay]
peach une pêche [pesh]
péage toll
peanuts: salted peanuts des cacahuètes salées
  [kahkah-wet sah-lay]
pear une poire [pwahr]
pebble un galet [gah-lay]
pedal la pédale [pay-dahl]
pedestrian un piéton [pee-yay-tōn]
  pedestrian crossing un passage pour piétons
  [pah-sahj . . .]
» *TRAVEL TIP: do not assume that cars will stop or even*
  slow down once you are on a pedestrian crossing; be
  extra cautious, especially with children
peg *(for tent)* un piquet de tente [pee-kay der tōnt]
  (clothes) une pince à linge [pāns ah lānj]
pelvis le bassin [bah-sān]
pen: have you got a pen? est-ce que vous avez un
  stylo? [. . . stee-loh]
pencil un crayon [kray-yōn]
penfriend un correspondant [kohres-pōn-dōn]
penicillin la pénicilline [paynee-see-leen]
penknife un canif [kah-neef]
pension guesthouse
pensioner un retraité [rertray-tay]
people les gens [jōn]
  how many people? combien de personnes? [pair-son]
pepper du poivre [pwahvr]
  green/red peppers des poivrons verts/rouges
  [pwah-vrōn vair, rooj]
peppermint une pastille de menthe [pahs-tee der mōnt]
per: per cent pour cent [poor sōn]
  per day/week/person par jour/semaine/personne
perfect parfait [par-fay]
  the perfect holiday des vacances idéales [vah-kōns
  eeday-ahl]
performance *(theatre etc)* une représentation
  [rerpray-zōn-tahs-yōn]
perfume un parfum [pahr-fān]
perhaps peut-être [per-taitr]
périphérique 'le périphérique' is the Paris ring road
period *(menstruation)* les règles [raygl]
  (time) une période [payr-yod]

perm une permanente [pairmah-nōnt]
permanent permanent [pairmah-nōn]
permit un permis [pair-mee]
permission une permission [pairmees-yōn]
person une personne [pair-son]
  in person en personne
personal personnel [pairsoh-nel]
  for personal use à usage personnel
  I'd like to make a personal call j'aimerais une
  communication avec préavis
  [... kohmoo-nee-kahs-yōn ah-vek pray-ah-vee]
pet un animal domestique
  [ahnee-mal dohmes-teek]
petrol de l'essence [ay-sōns]
  petrol station une station-service
  [stahs-yon-sair-vees]
  petrol gauge la jauge [johj] à essence
  petrol can le jerrycan d'essence
  petrol tank le réservoir
  YOU MAY SEE OR HEAR...
  super [soo-pair] = 4-star
  ordinaire [ohrdee-nair] = 2-star
  normale [nor-mahl] = 2-star
  give me 50F worth of 4-star donnez-moi pour
  cinquante francs de super [doh-nay-mwah poor
  sān-kōnt frōn der soo-pair]
» *TRAVEL TIP: the pump attendant will expect a tip if he
  gives your windscreen a wipe; routine checks such as
  'les niveaux' (oil and battery level) can be costly*
phone *see* **telephone**
photograph une photo
  would you take a photograph of us? est-ce que
  vous pouvez nous prendre en photo? [esker voo poo-vay
  noo prōndr ōn fohtoh]
piano un piano
pickpocket un pickpocket
picture *(photo)* une photo
picnic un pique-nique [peek-neek]
pie: pork pie un pâté en croûte [pah-tay ōn kroot]
» *TRAVEL TIP: pies as you know them do not exist in
  France; for a snack buy sandwiches in a café (look for
  the sign 'casse-croûte'), or buy bread (a 'baguette') and
  ham, pâté etc for a tasty 'pique-nique'*

piece: a piece of . . . un morceau de . . . [mohr-soh]

piétons pedestrians

pig un cochon [koh-shon]

pigeon un pigeon [pee-jon]

pile-up une collision en chaîne [kohleez-yon . . .]

pill: do you take the pill? est-ce que vous prenez la pilule? [esker voo prer-nay lah pee-lool]

pillion: on the pillion sur le siège arrière [soor ler see-yej ahr-yair]

pillow un oreiller [ohray-yay]

pin une épingle [ay-pangl]

pineapple un ananas [ahnah-nas]

pink rose [rohz]

pint = *approx.* un demi-litre [dermee-leetr]

» *TRAVEL TIP: 1 pint = 0.57 litre; if you ask for a beer, the standard measure is 0.33 l, slightly more than a half-pint (0.26 l)*

pipe une pipe [peep]

(for water) un tuyau [twee-yoh]

pipe tobacco du tabac [tah-bah] pour la pipe

piston un piston [pees-ton]

pity: it's a pity! c'est dommage! [doh-mahj]

place: is this place taken? est-ce que cette place [piahs] est prise?

do you know any good places to go? est-ce que vous connaissez des endroits [an-drwah] intéressants?

places debout standing room

places assises seated accommodation

plain simple [sanpl]

plain omelette une omelette nature [. . . nah-toor]

plain fabric du tissu uni [. . . oo-nee]

plan: we plan to . . . nous avons l'intention de . . . [nooz ah-von lantons-yon der]

plane un avion [ahv-yon]

plant *(flower etc)* une plante [plont]

(factory) une usine [oo-zeen]

plaster *(cast)* un plâtre [plahtr]

plastic: plastic bag un sac en plastique [sak on plahs-teek]

plate une assiette [ahs-yet]

platform: which platform? quel quai? [kel kay]

play jouer [joo-ay]

somewhere for the children to play un endroit où

les enfants peuvent jouer [ānn ōn-drwah oo layz ōnfōn perv joo-ay]

pleasant agréable [ahgray-ahbl]

please s'il vous plaît [seel voo play]

    could you please . . .? s'il vous plaît, est-ce que vous pouvez . . .? [. . . esker voo poo-vay]

    yes please oui, s'il vous plaît

    I am pleased to/with . . . je suis content de . . . [jer swee kōn-tōn der]

pleasure: it's a pleasure bien volontiers [bee-yān vohlōnt-yay]

    with pleasure avec plaisir [ah-vek play-zeer]

plenty: plenty of . . . beaucoup de . . . [boh-koo der]

    thank you, that's plenty merci, ça suffit [. . . sah soo-fee]

pliers des tenailles [ter-nah-ee]

plug (electrical) une prise [preez]

    (car) une bougie [boo-jee]

    (sink etc) la bonde [bōnd]

plum une prune [proon]

plumber un plombier [plōnb-yay]

    plumbing la plomberie [plōn-bree]

plus plus [ploos]

p.m.: 1 p.m. une heure de l'après-midi [oon err der lah-pray-mee-dee]

    7 p.m. sept heures du soir [set err doo swahr]

pneumonia une pneumonie [pnermoh-nee]

poached egg un oeuf poché [erf poh-shay]

pocket une poche [posh]

poids lourds heavy goods vehicles

point: could you point to it? est-ce que vous pouvez me l'indiquer? [. . . āndee-kay]

    four point six quatre virgule six [. . . veer-gool . . .]

    points (car) les vis platinées [vees plahtee-nay]

police la police [poh-lees]

    get the police! appelez la police! [ap-lay . . .]

    policeman un agent de police [ah-jōn der poh-lees]

    police station le commissariat [kohmee-sahr-yah]

    YOU MAY SEE . . .

    gendarmerie *police station (the 'gendarmes' operate outside large cities and on the roads)*

polish (for shoes) du cirage [see-rahj]

could you polish my shoes? est-ce que vous pouvez cirer mes souliers? [. . . see-ray may sool-yay]
polite poli [poh-lee]
politics la politique
polluted pollué [pohloo-ay]
polythene bag un sac en plastique
pool *(swimming)* une piscine [pee-seen]
poor pauvre [pohvr]
  (quality) médiocre [maid-yohkr]
popular populaire [pohpoo-lair]
  is it popular? *(place)* est-ce que c'est très fréquenté? [esker say tray fraykon-tay]
population la population [pohpoo-lahs-yon]
pork du porc [pohr]
port *(harbour)* un port [pohr]
  (drink) du porto
  to port à bâbord [ah bah-bohr]
porter un porteur [por-terr]
portrait un portrait [por-tray]
posh chic
possible possible [poh-seebl]
  could you possibly . . .? est-ce que vous pourriez . . .? [esker voo poor-yay]
post *(a letter)* poster [pohs-tay]
  what's the postage for . . .? il faut affranchir à combien pour . . .? [eel foh ahfron-sheer ah konb-yan poor]
  post box une boîte aux lettres [bwaht oh laitr]
  postcard une carte postale [. . . .pohs-tahl]
  post office la poste
  poste restante la poste restante [pohst res-tont]
» *TRAVEL TIP: you can telephone from any post office (open 8 am to 7 pm and 8–12 Sat mornings); in Paris the main post office is open 24 hrs a day, 7 days a week: 52 rue du Louvre; letter boxes are yellow; you may be asked to show your passport when collecting 'poste restante' items*
  YOU MAY SEE . . .
  colis *parcels*
  timbres *stamps*
poster un poster [pos-tair]
postman le facteur [fak-terr]
potato une pomme de terre [pom der tair]

pottery une poterie [pot-ree]
pound une livre [leevr]; NB: *the 'livre' is 500g*
» *TRAVEL TIP: conversion: pounds ÷ 11 × 5 = kilos*

pounds	1	3	5	6	7	8	9
kilos	0.4	1.4	2.3	2.7	3.2	3.6	4.1

poussez push
pour verser [vair-say]
　it's pouring il pleut à verse [eel pler ah vairs]
powder la poudre [poodr]
　powdered milk du lait en poudre
power cut une panne d'électricité
　[pan daylek-tree-see-tay]
power point une prise de courant [preez der koo-rōn]
prawns des crevettes roses [krer-vet rohz]
　prawn cocktail un cocktail de crevettes
prefer: I prefer . . . je préfère . . . [jer pray-fair]
pregnant: she is pregnant elle est enceinte [el ayt
　ōn-sānt]
prepare préparer [praypah-ray]
**prescription: can you make up this
　prescription?** est-ce que vous pouvez préparer cette
　ordonnance? [. . . praypah-ray set ohrdoh-nōns]
present: at present à présent [ah pray-zōn]
　here's a present for . . . voilà un cadeau pour . . .
　[vwahla ān kah-doh poor]
　it's for a present c'est pour offrir [say poor oh-freer]
president le président [prayzee-dōn]
press: could you press these? est-ce que vous pouvez
　repasser ces vêtements? [rerpah-say say vait-mōn]
pressing dry cleaning
pressure la pression [prays-yōn]
prêt-à-porter ready-to-wear
pretty joli [joh-lee]
　pretty expensive assez cher [ah-say . . .]
price le prix [pree]
　price list le tarif [tah-reef]
prière de . . . please . . .
priest un prêtre [praitr]
primeurs early produce
print *(photo)* une épreuve sur papier [ay-prerv soor
　pahp-yay]
　one print of each une épreuve de chaque [. . . shahk]
printed matter des imprimés [ānpree-may]

priorité (à droite) *right of way (to vehicles coming from the right)*

prison une prison [pree-zōn]

private: private beach/road plage/route privée [... pree-vay]

probably probablement [prohbah-bler-mōn]

problem un problème [proh-blem]

product un produit [proh-dwee]

profit un bénéfice [baynay-fees]

programme un programme *(on radio, TV)* une émission [aymees-yōn]

promise: I promise that ... je promets que ... [jer proh-may ker]

pronounce: how do you pronounce that? comment est-ce que ça se prononce? [kohmōnt esker sah ser proh-nōns]

propeller une hélice [ay-lees]

properly correctement [kohrek-ter-mōn]

property: it's my property ça m'appartient [sah mahpart-yān]

propriété privée *private, no trespassing*

protect protéger [prohtay-jay]

Protestant protestant [prohtes-tōn]

proud fier [fee-yair]

prove: I can prove it je peux le prouver [jer per ler proo-vay]

PTT Post Office

public: the public le public [poo-bleek]
  public convenience des toilettes [twah-let] publiques

» *TRAVEL TIP: public toilets are sometimes scarce and difficult to find; remember that cafés and bars always provide such facilities*

  public holidays les jours fériés [joor fayr-yay]

» *TRAVEL TIP: public holidays: Jan 1st; Easter; May 1st; Ascension Day; Whitsun and Monday; July 14th ('fête nationale'); Aug 15th ('l'Assomption'); Nov 1st ('la Toussaint'); Nov 11th (Remembrance Day); Dec 25th*

pudding un dessert [day-sair]

pull *(verb)* tirer [tee-ray]
  he pulled out in front of me il a déboîté juste devant moi [eel ah daybwah-tay joost der-vōn mwah]

pump une pompe [pōnp]
punctual ponctuel [pōnktoo-el]
puncture: I've had a puncture j'ai eu une crevaison
  [. . . krervay-zōn]
pure pur [poor]
purple violet [vee-yoh-let]
purpose: on purpose exprès [ex-pray]
purse un porte-monnaie [port-moh-nay]
push pousser [poo-say]
  push chair une poussette [poo-set]
put: where can I put . . .? où est-ce que je peux
  mettre . . .? [wesker jer per maitr]
  where have you put it? où est-ce que vous l'avez
  mis? [wesker voo lah-vay mee]
pyjamas pyjamas [peejah-mah]
quai at station: platform
quality la qualité [kahlee-tay]
quarantine: to stay in quarantine rester en
  quarantaine [. . . kahrōn-ten]
quarter: a quarter of an hour un quart d'heure
  [kahr-der]
quay un quai [kay]
question une question [kest-yōn]
queue une file d'attente [feel dah-tōnt]
» *TRAVEL TIP: don't necessarily expect orderly queuing*
quick rapide [rah-peed]
  that was quick c'était vite fait [say-tay veet fay]
  quickly rapidement [rahpeed-mon]
quiet tranquille [trōn-keel]
  be quiet! ne faites pas de bruit [ner fait pah der
  brwee]
quite *(fairly)* assez [ah-say]; *(very)* très [tray]
race une course [koors]
radiator un radiateur [rahd-yah-terr]
radio: on the radio à la radio [rahd-yoh]
rail: by rail en train [ōn trān]
rain la pluie [plwee]
  it's raining il pleut [pler]
  raincoat un imperméable [ānpair-may-ahbl]
ralentir slow down
rally *(car)* un rallye [rah-lee]
rape: I've been raped on m'a violée [ōn mah
  vee-yoh-lay]

....

rappel *on traffic signs: reminder*
rare rare [rahr]
  (steak) saignant [sayn-yōn]
rarely rarement [rahr-mōn]
rash une éruption de boutons [ayroops-yōn der boo-tōn]
raspberries des framboises [frōn-bwahz]
rat un rat [rah]
rate: do you have a special rate for
  children/students? est-ce que vous avez un tarif
  réduit pour les enfants/étudiants? [. . . ān tah-reef
  ray-dwee . . .]
  what's the rate for sterling? quel est le taux de la
  livre? [. . . toh der lah leevr]
rather *(fairly)* assez [ah-say]
  I'd rather je préférerais [pray-fair-ray]
raw cru [kroo]
razor un rasoir [rah-zwahr]
  razor blades des lames de rasoir [lahm . . .]
read: something to read quelque chose à lire [kel-ker
  shohz ah leer]
  would you read this for me? est-ce que vous pouvez
  me lire ça? [. . . mer leer sah]
ready: when will it be ready? ce sera prêt quand? [ser
  serah pray kōn]
  I'm not ready yet je ne suis pas encore prêt [jer ner
  swee pahz ōn-kor pray]
real *(leather etc)* véritable [vayree-tahbl]
  really? vraiment? [vray-mōn]
rear-view mirror le rétroviseur [raytroh-vee-zerr]
reasonable raisonnable [rayzoh-nahbl]
receipt: can I have a receipt? est-ce que je peux avoir
  une quittance? [. . . kee-tōns]
receive recevoir [rerser-vwahr]
recently récemment [raysah-mōn]
reception *(hotel)* la réception [rayseps-yōn]
  at reception à la réception
receptionist la réceptionniste [rayseps-yoh-neest]
recipe une recette [rer-set]
recommend: can you recommend . . .? est-ce que
  vous pouvez recommander . . .? [. . . rerkoh-mōn-day]
record *(music)* un disque [deesk]
red rouge [rooj]
reduction une réduction [raydooks-yōn]

refill une recharge [rer-shahrj]

refuse: I refuse ... je refuse ... [jer rer-fooz]

region: in this region dans cette région [dōn set rayj-yōn]

registered: I'd like to send this registered j'aimerais envoyer ça en recommandé [jaym-ray ōnvwah-yay sah ōn rerkoh-mōn-day]

remain rester [res-tay]

remember: do you remember? est-ce que vous vous rappelez? [esker voo voo rap-lay]
 I don't remember je ne me rappelle pas [jer ner mer rah-pel pah]

renseignements enquiries

rent: can I rent a car/bicycle? est-ce que je peux louer une voiture/bicyclette? [esker jer per loo-ay ...]
 YOU MAY HEAR ...
 une taxe kilométrique [tax keeloh-may-treek]
 = *mileage charge*

repair: can you repair it? est-ce que vous pouvez le réparer? [... ler raypah-ray]

repeat: could you repeat that slowly?
 est-ce que vous pouvez répéter lentement?
 [... raypay-tay lōnt-mōn]

replace *(give another)* remplacer [rōnplah-say]

reply une réponse [ray-pōns]

R.E.R. [air-er-air] *fast commuter train in the Greater Paris area*

rescue sauver [soh-vay]

reservation une réservation [rayzair-vahs-yōn]

reserve: can I reserve a seat? est-ce que je peux réserver une place? [esker jer per rayzair vay oon plahs]

responsible responsable [respōn-sahbl]

rest: the rest of le reste de [rest]
 I've come here for a rest je suis venu ici pour me reposer [... mer rerpoh-zay]

restaurant un restaurant [restoh-rōn]

» *TRAVEL TIP: it often pays to look for a place off the main road or high street; see the menu reader, pp 72–73*

retail price le prix de détail [pree der day-tah-ee]

retired: I am retired je suis à la retraite [jer sweez ah lah rer-trait]

return retourner [rertoor-nay]

a return/two returns to . . . un/deux aller-retour pour . . . [. . . ahlay rer-toor poor]

reverse gear la marche arrière [marsh ahr-yair]

reverse charge call une communication en PCV [kohmoo-nee-kahs-yōn ōn pay-say-vay]

rez-de-chaussée ground floor

rheumatism des rhumatismes [roomah-teesm]

rib une côte [koht]

rice du riz [ree]

rich riche [reesh]

ridiculous ridicule [reedee-kool]

riding: I'd like to go riding j'aimerais faire du cheval [jaym-ray fair doo sher-val]

right: that's right c'est juste [say joost]

you're right vous avez raison [vooz ah-vay ray-zōn]

on the right à droite [ah drwaht]

a right-hand drive car une voiture avec le volant à droite [. . . voh-lōn ah drwaht]

ring (on finger) une bague [bag]

ripe (fruit) mûr [moor]

river une rivière [reev-yair]

(main river) un fleuve [flerv]

road une route [root]

which is the road to . . .? quelle est la route pour . . .?

rob: I've been robbed on m'a dévalisé [ōn mah dayvah-lee-zay]

rock (stone) un rocher [roh-shay]

on the rocks avec de la glace [ah-vek der lah glahs]

roll (bread) the closest equivalent would be: un petit pain [per-tee pān]

Roman Catholic catholique [kahtoh-leek]

romantic romantique [rohmōn-teek]

roof le toit [twah]

roof rack la galerie [gal-ree]

room: there isn't enough room il n'y a pas assez de place [eeln-yah pahz ah-say der plahs]

have you got a single/double room? est-ce que vous avez une chambre pour une personne/deux personnes? [. . . oon shōnbr poor oon pair-son . . .]

for one night/two nights pour une nuit/deux nuits [poor oon nwee, der nwee]

YOU MAY THEN HEAR . . .

c'est complet [say kōn-play] sorry, we're full up

avec douche [doosh] *with shower*
avec cabinet de toilette [kahbee-nay der twah-let] *with private toilet*
avec salle de bain [sahl der ba̅n] *with private bathroom*
room number le numéro de la chambre [noomay-roh . . .]
room service le service des chambres [sair-vees . . .]
rope une corde [kord]
rose une rose [rohz]
rosé: a bottle of rosé une bouteille de rosé [boo-tay der roh-zay]
rough: the sea is rough la mer est mauvaise [lah mair ay moh-vayz]
roughly approximativement [ahproxee-mah-teev-mo̅n]
round (*circular*) rond [ro̅n]
  it's my round c'est ma tournée [say mah toor-nay]
  round trip un voyage aller et retour [. . . ah-lay ay rer-toor]
roundabout un rond-point [ro̅n-pwa̅n]
» *TRAVEL TIP: let cars coming from the right go first, even when you are on the roundabout*
route un itinéraire [eetee-nay-rair]
  which is the prettiest/fastest route? quel est l'itinéraire le plus agréable/rapide?
» *TRAVEL TIP: route planning will be easier with the yellow Michelin road maps (1 cm = 2 km); secondary roads are generally good, and a sensible alternative to M-ways*
routiers '*relais routiers' are good inexpensive restaurants catering primarily for transport drivers; don't hesitate to try them (look for a red and blue circular sign)*
rowing boat une barque [bark]
rubber du caoutchouc [kah-oo-tshoo]
  rubber band un élastique [aylass-teek]
rubbish les ordures [ohr-door]
  when is rubbish collected? quand est-ce qu'il y a le ramassage des ordures [ko̅nt eskeel yah le rahmah-sahj . . .]
  it's rubbish ça ne vaut rien [sahn voh ree-ya̅n]
rucksack un sac à dos [sak ah doh]
rudder le gouvernail [goovair-nah-ee]
rude impoli [a̅npoh-lee]

rum du rhum [rom]
run courir [koo-reer]
  (engine) marcher [mahr-shay]
  hurry, run! vite, dépêchez-vous! [veet
  daypay-shay-voo]
  I've run out of petrol/money je n'ai plus
  d'essence/d'argent [jer nay ploo day-sōns, dahr-jōn]
  he ran into my car il est rentré dans ma voiture [eel
  ay rōn-tray dōn . . .]
sables mouvants quicksand
sad triste [treest]
safe sans danger [sōn dōn-jay]
  will it be safe here? est-ce que ça ne risque rien ici?
  [. . . reesk ree-yān ee-see]
  is it safe to swim here? est-ce qu'on peut se baigner
  sans danger, ici?
  [eskōn per ser bayn-yay sōn dōn-jay . . .]
safety sécurité [saykoo-ree-tay]
  safety pin épingle de sureté [ay-pāngl der soor-tay]
sail une voile [vwahl]
  can we go sailing? est-ce qu'on peut faire de la voile?
  [eskōn per fair . . .]
» *TRAVEL TIP: check weather conditions at the
  'capitainerie' (harbour master's office)*
  sailor un marin [mah-rān]
salad une salade [sah-lad]
» *TRAVEL TIP: do not expect salad cream; salad is
  usually a green salad, served with a French dressing*
sale: is it for sale? est-ce qu'on peut l'acheter? [eskōn
  per lash-tay]
salle à manger dining room
salle d'attente waiting room
salmon le saumon [soh-mōn]
salt le sel
same le (la) même [maim]
  the same again, please la même chose, s'il vous plaît
  [lah maim shohz . . .]
  the same to you à vous pareillement [ah voo
  pahray-ee-mōn]
  it's all the same to me ça m'est égal [sah mait ay-gal]
sample *(a wine etc)* goûter [goo-tay]
  (of product) un échantillon [ayshōn-tee-yōn]
sand le sable [sahbl]

sandals des sandales [sōn-dahl]
sandwich un sandwich
  ham/cheese sandwich sandwich au jambon/
  fromage [. . . oh jōn-bon, froh-mahj]
» *TRAVEL TIP: not made with square sliced bread;*
  usually a section of French stick sliced lengthways
sanitary towel une serviette hygiénique [sairv-yet
  eej-yay-neek]
sans issue *no through way*
satisfactory satisfaisant [sahtees-fer-zōn]
Saturday samedi [sam-dee]
sauce la sauce [sohz]
  saucepan une casserole [kas-rohl]
saucer une soucoupe [soo-koop]
sauna un sauna [soh-nah]
sausage une saucisse [soh-sees]
  (cold) un saucisson [sohsee-sōn]
» *TRAVEL TIP: very different from the sausages you are*
  used to, except for Frankfurters; a 'saucisson'
  (salami-type sausage) with a French loaf will make a
  tasty picnic
save *(life)* sauver [soh-vay]
say: how do you say in French . . .? comment est-ce
  qu'on dit en français . . .? [koh-mōnt eskōn dee ōn
  frōn-say]
  what did he say? qu'est-ce qu'il a dit? [kes-keel ah
  dee]
scarf un foulard [foo-lar]
scenery le paysage [payee-zahj]
schedule *(timetable)* un horaire [oh-rair]
  (programme) un programme
  on schedule à l'heure [ah lerr]
  behind schedule en retard [rer-tahr]
  scheduled flight un vol régulier [vol raygool-yay]
school une école [ay-kol]
scissors une paire de ciseaux [pair der see-zoh]
Scotland l'Ecosse [ay-kos]
Scottish écossais [aykoh-say]
scrambled eggs des oeufs brouillés [er broo-yay]
scratch une éraflure [ayrah-floor]
scream: I heard somebody scream j'ai entendu
  quelqu'un crier [. . . kree-yay]
screw une vis [vees]

....

screwdriver un tournevis [toorner-vees]
sea la mer [mair]
  by the sea au bord de la mer [oh bor der . . .]
seafood des fruits de mer [frweed mair]
seafront le bord de mer [bor der mair]
search chercher [shair-shay]
  search party une expédition de secours
  [expay-dees-yōn der ser-koor]
seasick: I get/feel seasick j'ai le mal de mer [jay ler
  mal der mair]
seaside le bord de la mer [bor der lah mair]
season une saison [say-zōn]
  high/low season haute/basse saison
  [oht, bahs . . .]
  season ticket une carte d'abonnement [kart
  dahbon-mōn]
seasoning l'assaisonnement [ahsay-zon-mōn]
seat *(in train etc)* une place [plahs]
  (chair etc) un siège [see-yayj]
  is this somebody's seat? est-ce que cette place est
  occupée? [esker set plahs ayt ohkoo-pay]
  seat belt une ceinture de sécurité [sān-toor der
  saykoo-ree-tay]
» *TRAVEL TIP: wearing of seat belts compulsory outside*
  towns
  I'd like a window seat/a seat facing the engine
  j'aimerais une place près de la fenêtre/dans le sens de
  la marche [. . . pray der lah fer-naitr, dōn ler sōns der
  lah marsh]
seaweed des algues [alg]
second une seconde [ser-gōnd]
  (2nd) deuxième [derz-yem], *(date)* le deux [der]
  second hand d'occasion [dohkahz-yōn]
secretary une secrétaire [serkray-tair]
sedative un calmant [kal-mōn]
see: I see je vois [vwah]
  can I see the room? est-ce que je peux voir la
  chambre? [. . . vwahr . . .]
  have you seen . . .? est-ce que vous avez vu?
  [. . . voo]
  see you à bientôt [ah bee-yān-toh]
  see you tonight/tomorrow à ce soir/demain [ah ser
  swahr, der-mān]

seem: it seems that... il semble que...[eel sōnbl ker]
self: self-service self-service [... sair-vees]
  self-contained indépendant [āndāy-pōn-dōn]
sell vendre [vōndr]
send envoyer [ōnvwah-yay]
sens unique one way
sensitive sensible [sōn-seebl]
separate¹ séparer [saypah-ray]
  I'm separated je suis séparé de ma femme [jer swee
  saypah-ray der mah fam]
  (woman) je suis séparée de mon mari [... der mōn
  mah-ree]
separate² séparé
  can we pay separately? est-ce qu'on peut payer
  chacun pour soi? [eskōn per pay-yay shah-kān poor
  swah]
September: in September en septembre [sep-tōnbr]
serious sérieux [sair-yer]
  is it serious? *(injury etc)* est-ce que c'est grave?
  [... grahv]
serrez à droite keep to the right
serum *(for snake bite)* du sérum [say-rom]
serve: are you serving breakfast now? est-ce que
  vous servez le petit-déjeuner maintenant?
  [... sair-vay ...]
service le service [sair-vees]
  is the service charge included? est-ce que le service
  est compris?
service station une station-service [stahs-yōn
  sair-vees]
serviette une serviette [sairv-yet]
set *(fix)* fixer [fee-xay]
  (adjust) régler [ray-glay]
several plusieurs [plooz-yerr]
sew coudre [koodr]
shade: in the shade à l'ombre [ah lōnbr]
shake secouer [serkoo-ay]
» TRAVEL TIP: shaking hands ('se serrer la main') is
  common on meeting and leaving somebody
shallow peu profond [per proh-fōn]
shame: it's a shame c'est dommage [doh-mahj]
shampoo un shampooing [shōn-pwān]
  shampoo and set une mise en plis [meez ōn plee]

....

shandy une bière panachée [bee-yair pahnah-shay]
» *TRAVEL TIP: likely to be lager and lemonade*
shape la forme [form]
share partager [pahrtah-jay]
sharp *(blade etc)* coupant [koo-pōn]
shave: I must shave je dois me raser [. . . mer rah-zay]
  shaver un rasoir [rah-zwahr]
  shaving foam de la mousse à raser [moos ah rah-zay]
  shaving point une prise-rasoir [preez . . .]
she elle [el]
sheep un mouton [moo-tōn]
sheet un drap [drah]
  (paper) une feuille de papier [fer-ee der pahp-yay]
shelf une étagère [aytah-jair]
shell *(egg, nut)* la coquille [koh-kee]
  (sea) un coquillage [kohkee-yahj]
  shellfish des coquillages
shelter un abri [ah-bree]
  can we shelter here? est-ce que nous pouvons nous
  abriter ici? [. . . nooz ahbree-tay ee-see]
sherry un xérès [gzay-res]
shin le tibia [teeb-yah]
ship un bateau [bah-toh]
shirt une chemise [sher-meez]
  see **chest, collar**
shock un choc [shok]
  I got an electric shock from j'ai reçu une décharge
  électrique de [jay rer-soo oon day-sharj aylek-treek]
  shock-absorber un amortisseur [ahmor-tee-serr]
shoes des chaussures [shoh-soor]
» *TRAVEL TIP: shoe sizes*

UK	4	5	6	7	8	9	10	11
Continent	37	38	39	41	42	43	44	46

shop un magasin [mahgah-zān]
shopping: I've got some shopping to do j'ai des
  courses à faire [jay day koors ah fair]
» *TRAVEL TIP: opening hours: food shops usually 7.30 to
12.30 and 15.30 to 19.30; other shops 9 to 12 and 14 to
19; closing day gen. Mon (or half day Mon); bakers and
small grocers often open on Sun morning*
shore: on the shore sur le rivage [. . . ree-vahj]
short court [koor]
  I'm 3 short il m'en manque trois [eel mōn mōnk . . .]

short cut un raccourci [rahkoor-see]
shorts un short
shoulder l'épaule [ay-pohl]
shout crier [kree-yay]
show *(exhibition)* une exposition [expoh-zees-yōn]
   (theatre etc) un spectacle [spek-tahkl]
   please show me montrez-moi, s'il vous plaît
   [mōn-tray mwah . . .]
shower une douche [doosh]
shrimps des crevettes grises [krer-vet greez]
shrink: does it shrink? est-ce que ça rétrécit? [esker
   sah raytray-see]
shut fermer [fair-may]
   when do you shut? vous fermez à quelle heure? [voo
   fair-may ah kel err]
   shut up! taisez-vous! [tay-zay-voo]
shy timide [tee-meed]
sick malade [mah-lad]
   I feel sick je ne me sens pas bien [jer ner mer sōn pah
   bee-yān]
   he's been sick il a vomi [eel ah voh-mee]
side le côté
   on this side de ce côté
   on the other side de l'autre côté
   side lights les feux de position
   [fer der pohzees-yōn]
   side street une rue de traverse [roo der trah-vairs]
   by the side of the road au bord de la route [oh bor der
   lah root]
sight: out of sight hors de vue [or der voo]
   the sights of . . . les choses à voir dans . . . [lay shohz
   ah vwahr . . .]
   we'd like to go on a sightseeing tour nous
   voudrions faire une visite guidée [noo voodree-yōn fair
   oon vee-zet ghee-day]
sign *(road)* un panneau [pah-noh]
   (notice) un écriteau [aykree-toh]
signal: he didn't signal il n'a pas mis son clignotant
   [. . . mee sōn kleen-yoh-tōn]
signature une signature [seen-yah-toor]
silencer le silencieux [seelōns-yer]
silk la soie [swah]
silly stupide [stoo-peed]

silver: a silver chain une chaînette en argent [. . .onn ahr-jon]
similar semblable [son-blahbl]
simple simple [sanpl]
since: since last week depuis la semaine dernière [der-pwee . . .]
   since we arrived depuis notre arrivée
   since you want . . . puisque vous voulez . . . [pwees-ker . . .]
sincerely *see* **letter**
sing chanter [shon-tay]
single: single room une chambre pour une personne [shonbr poor oon pair-son]
   I'm single je suis célibataire [jer swee saylee-bah-tair]
   I'd like a single to j'aimerais un billet aller pour [. . . bee-yay ah-lay . . .]
sink *(boat)* couler [koo-lay]
   (kitchen) l'évier [ayv-yay]
Sir . . . Monsieur . . . [mers-yer]
   see **letter**
sister: my sister ma soeur [serr]
sit: can I sit here est-ce que je peux m'asseoir ici [. . . ah-swahr . . .]
   sit next to me asseyez-vous à côté de moi [ahsay-yay voo . . .]
size la taille [tie]
   (of shoes) la pointure [pwan-toor]
   do you have my size? est-ce que vous avez ma taille/pointure? [esker vooz ah-vay . . .]
   YOU MAY HEAR OR SEE . . .
   petit [per-tee] *small*
   moyen [mwah-yan] *medium*
   grand [gron] *large*
skates des patins [pah-tan]
   skating rink une patinoire [pahtee-nwahr]
skis des skis [skee]
   skiing boots des chaussures de ski [shoh-soor . . .]
   ski poles des bâtons de ski [bah-ton . . .]
   ski lift un remonte-pente [rer-mont-pont]
   ski run une piste [peest]
skid déraper [dayrah-pay]
skin la peau [poh]

skin-diving la plongée sous-marine [plōn-jay
 soo-mah-reen]
skirt une jupe [joop]
sky le ciel [see-yel]
sledge une luge [looj]
sleep: I can't sleep je ne peux pas dormir
 [. . . dor-meer]
 sleeper (train) un wagon-lit [vah-gōn-lee]
 sleeping bag un sac de couchage [sak der koo-shahj]
 sleeping pills des somnifères [somnee-fair]
sleeve une manche [mōnsh]
slice une tranche [trōnsh]
slides (photo) des diapositives [dee-yah-poh-zee-teev]
slippery glissant [glee-sōn]
slow lent [lōn]
 could you speak a little slower? est-ce que vous
 pouvez parler un peu plus lentement?
 [. . . ān per ploo lōnt-mōn]
small petit [per-tee]
 small change de la petite monnaie [per-teet
 moh-nay]
smallpox la variole [vahr-yohl]
smell: there's a funny smell il y a une odeur bizarre
 [eelyah oon oh-derr . . .]
 it smells ça sent [sah sōn]
smoke la fumée [foo-may]
 do you smoke? est-ce que vous fumez? [esker voo
 foo-may]
 can I smoke? est-ce que je peux fumer?
» TRAVEL TIP: smoking is prohibited in France in public
 buildings and on public transport, as well as in cinemas
snack un casse-croûte [kahs-kroot]
snake un serpent [sair-pōn]
S.N.C.F. the French Railways
snorkel un tuba [too-bah]
snow la neige [nej]
 powder snow la neige poudreuse [. . . poo-drerz]
so: it's so hot that. . . il fait si chaud que . . . [eel fay see
 shoh ker]
 not so much pas tant [pah-tōn]
 so so comme çi, comme ça [komsee-komsah]
soaked: we are soaked nous sommes trempés [noo
 som trōn-pay]

....

soap un savon [sah-vōn]
  soap powder *(washing)* du détergent [daytair-jōn]
socks une paire de chaussettes [pair der shoh-set]
soda water de l'eau [oh] de seltz
soft doux [doo]
  soft drinks des boissons sans alcool [bwah-sōn sōnz
al-kol]
soldes *sale*
sole *(fish)* une sole
  (shoe) une semelle [ser-mel]
  could you put new soles on these? est-ce que vous
pouvez ressemeler ces chaussures? [. . . rers-mer-lay
say shoh-soor]
some: some places certains endroits [sair-tān . . .]
  can I have some? est-ce que je peux en avoir? [esker
jer per ōnn ah-vwahr]
  some bread du [doo] pain; **some beer** de la [der lah]
bière; **some crisps** des [day] chips
  can I have some more? est-ce que je peux en avoir
plus? [. . . ōnn ah-vwahr ploos]
somebody quelqu'un [kel-kān]
something quelque chose [kel-ker shohz]
sometimes quelquefois [kelker-fwah]
somewhere quelque part [kel-ker par]
son: my son mon fils [fees]
song une chanson [shōn-sōn]
sonnez *please ring*
soon bientôt [bee-yān-toh]
  as soon as possible dès que possible [day ker
poh-seebl]
  sooner plus tôt [ploo toh]
sore: it's sore ça fait mal [sah fay mal]
  I have a sore throat j'ai mal à la gorge [jay mal ah
lah gohrj]
sorry: I'm sorry excusez-moi [exkoo-zay-mwah]
sort: what sort of? quelle sorte de? [kel sort der]
  will you sort the problem out? est-ce que vous
pouvez arranger ça? [. . . ahrōn-jay sah]
sortie de camions *lorries crossing*
  sortie de secours *emergency exit*
sound: it sounds interesting ça a l'air intéressant
[sah ah lair . . .]
soup une soupe [soop]

sour aigre [aigr]
sous-sol *basement*
south le sud [sood]
   South Africa l'Afrique du Sud [ah-freek . . .]
souvenir un souvenir [soov-neer]
spade *(for beach)* une pelle [pel]
Spain l'Espagne [es-pan]
   in Spain en Espagne [ōnn . . .]
   Spanish espagnol [espan-yol]
spanner une clé anglaise [klay ōn-glayz]
spare: **spare parts** des pièces de rechange [pee-yes der rer-shōnj]
   spare wheel la roue de secours [roo der ser-koor]
sparking plugs les bougies [boo-jee]
speak: **do you speak English?** est-ce que vous parlez anglais? [esker voo par-lay ōn-glay]
   is there somebody who speaks English? est-ce qu'il y a quelqu'un qui parle anglais? [. . . kel-kān kee parl ōn-glay]
   I don't speak French je ne parle pas français [jer ner parl pah frōn-say]
special spécial [spays-yal]
specialist un spécialiste [spays-yah-leest]
specially spécialement [spays-yal-mōn]
spectacles des lunettes [loo-net]
speed la vitesse [vee-tes]
   he was speeding il allait trop vite [eel ah-lay troh veet]
   speed limit une limitation de vitesse [leemee-tahs-yōn . . .]
speedometer le compteur de vitesse [kōn-terr]
» *TRAVEL TIP: speed limit: in towns 60 km/h (38 mph); on roads 90 km/h (56 mph); on dual carriageways 110 km/h (70 mph); on M-ways 130 km/h (81 mph)*
spell: **how do you spell it?** comment ça s'écrit? [koh-mōn sah say-kree]
spend *(money)* dépenser
   (time) passer
spices des condiments [kōndee-mōn]
   is it spicy? est-ce que c'est très épicé? [. . . aypee-say]
spider une araignée [ahrain-yay]
spirits des spiritueux [spee-ree-too-er]
spoon une cuillère [kwee-yair]

....

sprain une entorse [on-tohrs]
   I've sprained my ankle je me suis foulé la cheville
   [jer mer swee foo-lay . . .]
spring *(season)* le printemps [pran-ton]
   (metal) un ressort [rer-sor]
   (water) une source [soors]
square *(in town)* une place [plahs]
   2 square metres deux mètres carrés [. . . maitr
   kah-ray]
staff le personnel [pairsoh-nel]
stairs les escaliers [eskahl-yay]
stalls: 2 stalls deux orchestre [derz or-kestr]
stamp: 2 stamps for Great Britain deux timbres
   [tanbr] pour la Grande-Bretagne
» *TRAVEL TIP: you can buy stamps from many*
   newsagents and some cafés; look for the sign
   'tabacs-journaux' or 'tabac'
stand *(at fair)* un stand [ston]
standard normal
star une étoile [ay-twahl]
starboard: to starboard à tribord [ah tree-bor]
start commencer [kohmon-say] .
   my car won't start ma voiture ne démarre pas [mah
   vwah-toor ner day-mar pah]
   when does it start? ça commence quand? [sah
   koh-mons kon]
starter *(car)* le démarreur [daymah-rerr]
   (dish) une entrée [on-tray]
starving: I'm starving je meurs de faim [jer merr der
   fan]
station la gare [gar]
   (underground) la station de métro [stahs-yon . . .]
stationer's une papeterie [pahpet-ree]
stationnement parking
statue une statue [stah-too]
stay: we enjoyed our stay nous avons fait un très bon
   séjour [. . . say-joor]
   stay there restez là [res-tay lah]
   I'm staying at . . . je séjourne à . . . [say-joorn]
steak un steak [stek]
   YOU MAY HEAR . . .
   à point [ah pwan] *medium*
   bien cuit [bee-yan kwee] *well done*

saignant [sayn-yōn] *rare*
steal voler [voh-lay]
steep *(slope)* raide [red]
steering *(car)* la direction [deereks-yōn]
  steering wheel le volant [voh-lōn]
step *(stairs)* une marche [marsh]
stereo stéréo [stay-ray-oh]
sterling: in sterling en livres sterling [ōn leevr
  stair-ling]
stewardess une hôtesse [oh-tes]
sticking plaster un pansement adhésif [pōns-
  mōn ahday-zeef]
sticky poisseux [pwah-ser]
stiff dur [door]
still: keep still restez tranquille [res-tay trōn-keel]
  I'm still here je suis encore là [jer swee ōn-kor . . .]
stockings des bas [bah]
stolen: my wallet's been stolen on m'a volé mon
  portefeuille [ōn mah voh-lay . . .]
stomach l'estomac [estoh-mah]
  I've got a stomach-ache j'ai mal au ventre [jay mal
  oh vōntr]
  **have you got something for an upset
  stomach?** est-ce que vous avez quelque chose pour les
  maux de ventre? [. . . moh der vōntr]
stone une pierre [pee-yair]
» *TRAVEL TIP: weight: 1 stone = 6.35 kg*
stop s'arrêter [. . . ahray-tay]
  do you stop near . . .? est-ce que vous vous arrêtez
  près de . . .? [esker voo vooz ahray-tay pray der]
  stop over une escale [es-kahl]
storm une tempête [tōn-pet]
straight droit [drwah]
  (whisky etc) sec
  go straight on continuez tout droit [kōntee-
  noo-ay too drwah]
  straight away immédiatement [eemayd-yat-mōn]
strange bizarre
stranger un inconnu [ānkoh-noo]
  I'm a stranger here je ne suis pas d'ici [jer ner swee
  pah dee-see]
strap une courroie [koo-rwah]
strawberries des fraises [frayz]

street une rue [roo]
  a **street map** of un plan de [plōn]
strike une grève [graiv]
string de la ficelle [fee-sel]
stroke: he's had a **stroke** il a eu une attaque
  [. . . ah-tak]
strong fort [for]
stuck coincé [kwān-say]
student un étudiant [aytood-yōn]
stung: I've been **stung** by . . . j'ai été piqué par . . .
  [jay ay-tay pee-kay par]
stupid stupide [stoo-peed]
suburbs la banlieue [bōnl-yer]
successful: was it **successful**? est-ce que ça a réussi?
  [esker sah ah ray-oo-see]
such: such a lot of . . . tant de . . . [tōn der]
suddenly subitement [soobeet-mōn]
suffer: he's **suffering** from il souffre de [soofr der]
sugar du sucre [sookr]
» *TRAVEL TIP: sugar in lumps is the rule; if you want
  granulated sugar, ask for 'du sucre en poudre'* [sookr ōn
  poodr]
suit *(man's)* un complet [kōn-play]
  (woman's) un tailleur [tah-yerr]
suitable: it's not **suitable** ça ne convient pas [sah ner
  kōnv-yān pah]
suitcase une valise [vah-leez]
summer l'été [ay-tay]
sun le soleil [soh-lay]
  in the sun au soleil
  out of the sun à l'abri du soleil [ah lah-bree . . .]
  sunbathe se bronzer [ser brōn-zay]
  sunburn un coup de soleil [koo . . .]
  sunglasses des lunettes de soleil [loo-net . . .]
  sunstroke une insolation [ānsoh-lahs-yōn]
  suntan oil de l'huile solaire [weel soh-lair]
Sunday dimanche [dee-mōnsh]
supermarket un supermarché [soopair-mar-shay]
» *TRAVEL TIP: often open on Sun mornings*
supper le souper [soo-pay]
» *TRAVEL TIP: supper is not served, as lunch is a main
  meal and dinner is served around 7 or 8 pm*
sure: I'm not **sure** je ne suis pas sûr [. . . soor]

sure! bien entendu! [bee-yann onton-doo]
  are you sure? vous êtes sûr? [vooz ayt soor]
surfboard une planche de surf [plonsh der soorf]
surfing: to go surfing faire du surf [fair du soorf]
surname le nom de famille [non der fah-mee]
sweat transpirer [tronspee-ray]
sweater un pull [pool]
sweet *(dessert)* un dessert [day-sair]
  it's too sweet c'est trop sucré [. . . soo-kray]
swerve: I had to swerve j'ai dû donner un coup de
  volant [jay doo doh-nay an koo der voh-lon]
swim: I can't swim je ne sais pas nager [jer ner say pah
  nah-jay]
  I'm going for a swim je vais me baigner [jer vay mer
  bayn-yay]
  swimming costume un maillot de bain [mah-yoh der
  ban]
  swimming trunks un slip de bain
  swimming pool une piscine [pee-seen]
switch un interrupteur [antay-roop-terr]
  switch the light on/off allumez/éteignez la lumière
  [ahloo-may, aytayn-yay . . .]
  switchboard le standard [ston-dar]
Swiss suisse [swees]
Switzerland la Suisse [swees]
tabac-journaux *tobacconist and newsagent*
table: a table for 4 une table pour quatre [oon tahbl
  poor kahtr]
  table wine du vin ordinaire [van ohrdee-nair]
taille *size*
take prendre [prondr]
  can I take this with me? est-ce que je peux emporter
  ça? [. . . onpohr-tay . . .]
  take me to the airport emmenez-moi à l'aéroport
  [onm-nay mwah . . .]
  can I take you out tonight? est-ce que vous voulez
  sortir avec moi ce soir? [. . . sohr-teer ah-vek mwah ser
  swahr]
  is this seat taken? est-ce que cette place est prise?
  [. . . set plahs ay preez]
talcum powder du talc
talk parler [par-lay]
tall grand [gron]

....

tampons des tampons hygiéniques [tonpon
   eej-yay-neek]
tan le bronzage [bron-zahj]
   I want to get a tan je veux bronzer [jer ver bron-zay]
tank le réservoir [rayzair-vwahr]
tap le robinet [rohbee-nay]
tape une bande magnétique [bond mahn-yay-teek]
tape-recorder un magnétophone [mahn-yay-toh-fon]
tariff le tarif [tah-reef]
taste: what does it taste like? quel goût ça a? [kel goo
   sah ah]
   can I taste it? est-ce que je peux goûter? [esker jer per
   goo-tay]
   it tastes horrible/very nice c'est affreux/
   délicieux [sayt ah-frer, daylees-yer]
taxi un taxi [tah-xee]
   will you get me a taxi? est-ce que vous pouvez
   m'appeler un taxi? [. . . map-lay an tah-xee]
   where can I get a taxi? où est-ce que je peux trouver
   un taxi?
   stop here arrêtez-vous ici [ahray-tay-voo ee-see]
   YOU MAY SEE . . .
   tête de station *taxi stance*
» *TRAVEL TIP: don't forget to tip (about 10%)*
***T.C.F.** = Touring Club de France, similar to AA or RAC*
tea le thé [tay]
   could I have a cup of tea? est-ce que je peux avoir un
   thé?
   a pot of tea for 2 une théière pour deux [tay-yair poor
   der]
   YOU MAY THEN HEAR . . .
   un thé lait [tay lay] *tea with milk*
   un thé citron [tay see-tron] *lemon tea*
» *TRAVEL TIP: tea is not automatically served with milk*
teach: could you teach me French? est-ce que vous
   pouvez m'apprendre le français? [. . . mah-prondr ler
   fron-say]
teacher le professeur [prohfay-serr]
teinturerie dry cleaner's
telegram: I want to send a telegram je veux envoyer
   un télégramme [. . . onvwah-yay an taylay-gram]
telephone le téléphone [taylay-fon]
   (where) can I make a phone-call? (où) est-ce que je

peux téléphoner? [. . . taylay-foh-nay]
can I speak to . . .? est-ce que je peux parler à . . .?
[esker jer per pahr-lay ah]
could you get this number for me? est-ce que vous
pouvez m'appeler ce numéro? [. . . map-lay ser
noomay-roh]
extension . . . poste numéro . . . [pohst noomay-roh]
telephone directory l'annuaire du téléphone
[ahnoo-air . . .]
YOU MAY HEAR . . .
qui est à l'appareil? *who's speaking?*
c'est un faux numéro *sorry wrong number*
la ligne est occupée *the line is engaged*
ça ne répond pas *there is no answer*
ne quittez pas, je vous passe . . . *hold the line, I'm
putting you through to . . .*
» *TRAVEL TIP: you can phone from most cafés: pay at
counter or you may have to buy a 'jeton'* [jer-tōn] *(token)
which you insert in the pay phone; there are now more
call boxes, esp. in Paris (grey colour): insert coin (50
centimes for local call) before lifting receiver; if you get
somebody to call you back from the UK: 010 33 plus
town prefix without the 0; see numbers on last page*
television: I'd like to watch television
j'aimerais regarder la télévision [jaim-ray rergahr-day
lah taylay-veez-yōn]
tell: could you tell me where/if . . .? est-ce que vous
pouvez me dire où/si . . .? [esker voo poo-vay mer deer
oo, see]
temperature la température [tōnpay-rah-toor]
he's got a temperature il a de la température
temporary provisoire [prohve-zwahr]
tennis: do you play tennis? est-ce que vous jouez au
tennis? [. . . joo-ay oh tay-nees]
tennis court un court de tennis [koor . . .]
tennis racquet une raquette de tennis [rah-ket . . .]
tennis ball une balle de tennis [bahl . . .]
tent une tente [tōnt]
terminus le terminus [tairmee-noos]
terrible terrible [tay-reebl]
(bad) affreux [ah-frer]
terrific fantastique [fōntahs-teek]
than: bigger than . . . plus grand que . . . [. . . ker]

thanks merci [mair-see]; **no thanks** non merci
  thank you very much merci beaucoup [. . . boh-koo]
  thank you for your help merci de votre aide
that ce (cette) [ser, set]
  that man/plane cet homme/avion [set . . .]
  I would like that one j'aimerais celui-là (celle-là)
  [. . . serlwee-lah, sel-lah]
  and that? et ça? [. . . sah]
  I think that . . . je crois que . . . [. . . ker]
the le (la), les [ler, lah, lay]
  the children les enfants [layz . . .]
  the airport l'aéroport
theatre le théâtre [tay-ahtr]
their leur, leurs [lerr]
  their car leur voiture, **their children** leurs enfants
  it's their suitcase, it's theirs c'est leur valise, c'est la
  leur
them: with them avec eux (elles) [. . . er, el]
  we didn't see them nous ne les avons pas vus
  [. . . lay . . .]
  we gave them the money nous leur avons donné
  l'argent [. . . lerr . . .]
then ensuite [on-sweet]
there là [lah]
  how do I get there? comment est-ce qu'on y va?
  [koh-mon eskonn ee vah]
  there is, there are il y a [eel-yah]
  there isn't, there aren't il n'y a pas de [eeln-yah pah
  der]
  is there a bus? est-ce qu'il y a un bus?
  [eskeel-yah . . .]
  there you are *(giving something)* voilà [vwah-lah]
these: these apples ces pommes [say . . .]
  can I take these? est-ce que je peux prendre ceux-ci
  (celles-ci)? [. . . ser-see, sel-see]
they ils (elles) [eel, el]
thick épais [ay-pay]
thief un voleur [voh-ler]
thigh la cuisse [kwees]
thin mince [mans]
thing une chose [shohz]
  I've lost all my things j'ai perdu toutes mes affaires
  [jay pair-doo toot mayz ah-fair]

think: I'll think it over je vais y réfléchir [jer vayz ee
 rayflay-sheer]
 I think so je crois [jer krwah]
 I don't think so je ne crois pas
 I think that . . . je crois que . . .
third troisième [trwahz-yem]
thirsty: I'm thirsty j'ai soif [jay swahf]
this ce (cette) [ser, set]
 this man/plane cet homme/avion [set . . .]
 I would like this one j'aimerais celui-ci (celle-ci)
 [serlwee-see, sel-see]
 this is my wife/Mr . . . voici ma femme/Monsieur . . .
 [vwah-see . . .]
 this is . . . c'est . . . [say]
 is this . . .? est-ce que c'est . . .? [esker say]
 and this? et ça? [. . . sah]
those: those people ces gens [say jon]
 how much are those? combien coûtent ceux-ci
 (celles-ci)? [. . . ser-see, sel-see]
thread du fil [feel]
three trois [trwah]
throat la gorge [gorj]
 throat lozenges des pastilles pour la gorge
 [pas-tee . . .]
through à travers [ah trah-vair]
throw lancer [lon-say]
thumb le pouce [poos]
thunder le tonnerre [toh-nair]
 thunderstorm un orage [oh-rahj]
Thursday jeudi [jer-dee]
ticket un billet [bee-yay]
tie *(necktie)* une cravate [krah-vat]
tight *(clothes):* **they're too tight** ils sont trop justes
 [. . . joost]
tights des collants [koh-lon]
time: what's the time? quelle heure il est?
 [kayl err eel ay]
 at what time? à quelle heure?
 I haven't got time je n'ai pas le temps [. . . ler ton]
 for the time being pour le moment [. . . moh-mon]
 this time cette fois [set fwah]
 last/next time la dernière/prochaine fois [dairn-yair,
 proh-shain fwah]

....

3 times trois fois
have a good time! amusez-vous bien!
[ahmoo-zay-voo bee-yāñ]
HOW TO TELL THE TIME:
it's 2 am/pm c'est deux heures du matin/de l'après-
midi [say derz err doo mahtāñ, der lah-pray-mee-dee]
at 7 pm à sept heures du soir [ah set err doo swahr]
2.05 deux heures cinq
2.15 deux heures et quart [. . . ay kar]
2.30 deux heures et demie [. . . ay der-mee]
2.40 trois heures moins vingt [. . . mwāñ vāñ]
2.45 trois heures moins le quart [. . . mwāñ ler kar]
timetable un horaire [oh-rair]
tin une boîte [bwaht]
  tin-opener un ouvre-boîte [oovr-bwaht]
tip: is the tip included? est-ce que le pourboire est
  compris? [. . . poor-bwahr . . .]
» *TRAVEL TIP: tip usherettes (about 2F), taxi drivers, and*
  lavatory attendants (about 50 centimes)
tired: I'm tired je suis fatigué [fahtee-gay]
tirez pull
tissues des Kleenex
to: to Paris à Paris
  to our friends' chez [shay] nos amis
  to England/Scotland en [oñ] Angleterre/Ecosse
toast un toast [tohst]
tobacco du tabac [tah-bah]
tobacconist's un bureau de tabac [boo-roh der tah-bah]
today aujourd'hui [ohjoor-dwee]
toe le doigt de pied [dwah der pee-yay]
together: we're together nous sommes ensemble
  [. . . oñ-soñbl]
toilet: where are the toilets? où sont les toilettes? [oo
  soñ lay twah-let]
  I have to go to the toilet je dois aller aux toilettes [jer
  dwahz ah-lay oh . . .]
  there's no toilet paper il n'y a pas de papier
  hygiénique [. . . pahp-yay eej-yay-neek]
tomato une tomate [toh-mat]
  tomato juice un jus [joo] de tomate
  tomato ketchup *you will not find tomato ketchup ('le*
  ketchup' [ket-sherp]) in a French restaurant, unless it's
  a fast food establishment

tomorrow demain [der-mān]
  tomorrow morning/afternoon/evening
  demain matin/après-midi/soir [der-mān mah-tān,
  ahpray-mee-dee, swahr]
  the day after tomorrow après-demain
  [ahpray-der-mān]
ton une tonne [ton]
  » *TRAVEL TIP: 1 ton = 1,016 kilos*
tongue la langue [lōng]
tonic *(water)* un schweppes [shveps]
tonight ce soir [ser swahr]
tonne une tonne [ton]
  » *TRAVEL TIP: 1 tonne = 1,000 kg = metric ton*
tonsils les amygdales [ahmee-dahl]
tonsillitis une angine [ōn-jeen]
too trop [troh]
  that's too much c'est trop
  too much . . ., too many . . . trop de . . .
tool un outil [oo-tee]
tooth une dent [dōn]
  I've got toothache j'ai mal aux dents [jay mal oh dōn]
  toothbrush une brosse à dents [brohs ah dōn]
  toothpaste du dentifrice [dōntee-frees]
top: on top of sur [soor]
  on the top floor au dernier étage [oh dairn-
  yair ay-tahj]
  at the top en haut [ōn oh]
total le total [toh-tal]
tough dur [door]
tour une excursion [exkoors-yōn]
  we'd like to go on a tour of . . . nous aimerions
  visiter . . . [noozaymer-yōn veezee-tay]
  we're touring around nous visitons la région [noo
  veezee-tōn lah rayj-yōn]
tourist: I'm a tourist je suis un touriste
  [. . . too-reest]
  tourist office le syndicat d'initiative [sāndee-kah
  deenees-yah-teev]
toutes directions through traffic
tow: can you give me a tow? est-ce que vous pouvez
  me remorquer? [. . . mer rermohr-kay]
  towrope une corde de dépannage [kord der
  daypah-nahj]

towards: he was coming straight towards me il
venait droit vers moi [. . . drwah vair mwah]
towel une serviette [sairv-yet]
town une ville [veel]
   in town en ville
   would you take me into the town? est-ce que vous
pouvez m'emmener en ville?
traditional traditionnel [trahdees-yoh-nel]
traffic la circulation [seerkoo-lahs-yōn]
   traffic lights les feux [fer]
   traffic policeman un agent de la circulation
[ah-jōn . . .]
train un train [trāñ]
» *TRAVEL TIP: you may have to punch your ticket before
boarding the train: look for orange-coloured machines
located on platforms or for the notice 'compostez votre
billet'; children under 10 pay half-fare, go free under 4;
there are extra charges on some inter-city trains*
traiteur delicatessen, caterers
tranquillizers des tranquillisants [trōñkee-lee-zōn]
translate: would you translate that for me?
est-ce que vous pouvez me traduire ça? [. . . mer
trah-dweer sah]
transmission *(of car)* la transmission [trōñsmees-yōn]
travaux roadworks
travel agent's une agence de voyage [ah-jōns der
voh-yahj]
traveller's cheque un traveller's cheque
tree un arbre [ahrbr]
trip ūn voyage [voh-yahj]
   (short tour, drive) une excursion [exkoors-yōn]
   we want to go on a trip to . . . nous voulons faire une
excursion à . . .
trouble: I'm having trouble with . . . j'ai des ennuis
avec . . . [jay dayz ōnn-wee ah-vek]
trousers un pantalon [pōntah-lōn]
true vrai [vray]
trunks *(swimming)* un slip de bain [. . . der bāñ]
try essayer [essay-yay]
   can I try it on? est-ce que je peux l'essayer?
T-shirt un T-shirt
t.t.c. = *toutes taxes comprises (inclusive of any duties)*
Tuesday mardi [mahr-dee]

tunnel un tunnel [too-nel]
turn: where do we turn off? où est-ce qu'il faut tourner? [wes-keel foh toor-nay]
 he turned without indicating il a tourné sans mettre le clignotant [. . . ler kleen-yoh-tōn]
T.V.A. [tay-vay-ah] *VAT*
twice deux fois [der fwah]
twin beds des lits jumeaux [lee joo-moh]
 twin room une chambre à deux lits [shōnbr ah der lee]
two deux [der]
typewriter une machine à écrire [mah-sheen ah ay-kreer]
typical typique [tee-peek]
tyre un pneu [pner]
 I need a new tyre il me faut un pneu neuf [eel mer foh ān pner nerf]
» *TRAVEL TIP: tyre pressures*

lb/sq in	18	20	22	24	26	28	30
kg/sq cm	1.3	1.4	1.5	1.7	1.8	2	2.1

ugly laid [lay]
ulcer un ulcère [ool-sair]
 (in mouth) un aphte [ahft]
umbrella un parapluie [pahrah-plwee]
uncle: my uncle mon oncle [ōnkl]
uncomfortable inconfortable [ānkōn-for-tahbl]
unconscious: he is unconscious il a perdu connaissance [eel ah pair-doo kohnay-sōns]
under sous [soo]
 he's under 12 il a moins de douze ans [eel ah mwan der . . .]
underdone pas assez cuit [pahz ah-say kwee]
underexposed sous-exposé [soozex-poh-zay]
underground *(rail)* le métro [may-troh]
 see **métro**
understand: I don't understand je ne comprends pas [jer ner kōn-prōn pah]
 do you understand? est-ce que vous comprenez? [. . . kōnprer-nay]
undo défaire [day-fair]
United States les Etats-Unis [aytahz-oo-nee]
university l'université [oonee-vair-see-tay]
unlock ouvrir [oo-vreer]

....

until jusqu'à [joos-kah]
   until July jusqu'en juillet [joos-kōn . . .]
unusual inhabituel [eenah-bee-too-el]
up en haut [ōn oh]
   he's not up yet il n'est pas encore levé [eel nay pahz ōn-kor ler-vay]
upside down à l'envers [ah lōn-vair]
upstairs en haut [ōn oh]
urgent urgent [oor-jōn]
us nous [noo]
USA les USA [oo-es-ah]
use: can I use . . .? est-ce que je peux utiliser . . .? [esker jer per ootee-lee-zay]
useful utile [oo-teel]
usual habituel [ahbee-too-el]
   as usual comme d'habitude [kom dahbee-tood]
   usually d'habitude [dahbee-tood]
U-turn un demi-tour [der-mee-toor]
vacancy: do you have any vacancies? est-ce que vous avez de la place? [. . . der lah plahs]
vacate *(room)* libérer [leebay-ray]
vaccination un vaccin [vak-sān]
vacuum flask un thermos [tair-mohs]
valid: how long is it valid for? c'est valable combien de temps? [say vah-lahbl kōnb-yān der tōn]
valley une vallée [vah-lay]
valuable: it's valuable ça a de la valeur [. . . vah-lerr]
   will you look after my valuables? est-ce que vous pouvez me garder mes objets de valeur? [. . . mer gahr-day mayz ob-jay der vah-lerr]
value la valeur [vah-lerr]
valves *(of car)* les soupapes [soo-pap]
van une camionnette [kahm-yoh-net]
vanilla *(ice-cream)* à la vanille [ah lah vah-nee]
varicose veins des varices [vah-rees]
veal du veau [voh]
vegetables des légumes [lay-goom]
vegetarian végétarien [vayjay-tahr-yān]
vendre: à vendre for sale
ventilator un ventilateur [vōntee-lah-terr]
very très [tray]
   very much beaucoup [boh-koo]
view la vue [voo]

via par
village un village [vee-lahj]
vine une vigne [veen]
vinegar du vinaigre [vee-naigr]
vineyard un vignoble [veen-yohbl]
vintage: a good vintage une bonne année [bon ah-nay]
violent violent [vee-yoh-lōn]
virages bends
visibility la visibilité [veezee-bee-lee-tay]
visit visiter [veezee-tay]
  visitor une visite [vee-zeet]
vitesse limitée à . . . speed limit . . .
voice la voix [vwah]
voie 6 platform 6 ('voie' is the actual track, but corresponds to the British system of platform numbering)
voltage le voltage [vol-tahj]
  is it 220V? est-ce que c'est du deux cent vingt volts? [. . . doo der sōn vān vohlt]
waist la taille [tie]
» TRAVEL TIP: waist measurements

UK	24	26	28	30	32	34	36	38
Continent	61	66	71	76	80	87	91	97

wait: will we have to wait long? est-ce qu'il faudra attendre longtemps? [eskeel foh-drah ah-tōndr lōn-tōn]
  wait for me! attendez-moi! [ahtōn-day-mwah]
  I'm waiting for j'attends [jah-tōn]
waiter le serveur [sair-verr]
  waiter! s'il vous plaît! [seel voo play]
waitress la serveuse [sair-verz]
  waitress! s'il vous plaît! [seel-voo play]
wake: will you wake me up at 7.30? est-ce que vous pouvez me réveiller à 7.30? [. . . mer rayvay-yay . . .]
Wales le Pays de Galles [payee der gal]
walk: can we walk there? est-ce qu'on peut y aller à pied? [. . . ee ah-lay ah pee-yay]
  are there any good walks around here? est-ce qu'il y a des promenades intéressantes dans les environs? [. . . day prohm-nad āntay-ray-sōnt . . .]
  walking shoes des chaussures de marche [shoh-soor der marsh]

walking stick une canne [kan]
wall le mur [moor]
wallet un portefeuille [pohrter-fer-ee]
want: I want . . . je voudrais . . . [jer voo-dray]
  I want to talk to . . . je voudrais parler à . . . *(note that you can say 'je veux', but 'je voudrais' is more courteous)*
  we want . . . nous voulons . . . [noo voo-lōn]
  he wants . . . il veut . . . [eel ver]
  what do you want? qu'est-ce que vous voulez? [kesker voo voo-lay]
  I don't want . . . je ne veux pas . . . [jer ner ver pah]
war la guerre [gair]
warm chaud [shoh]
warn avertir [ahvair-teer]
wash: can you wash these for me? est-ce que vous pouvez me laver ça? [. . . mer lah-vay sah]
  where can I wash? où est-ce que je peux me laver? [wesker jer per mer lah-vay]
  washable lavable [lah-vahbl]
  washbasin un lavabo [lahvah-boh]
  washing powder de la poudre à lessive [poodr ah lay-seev]
  washing up liquid du détergent pour la vaisselle [daytair-jōn poor lah vay-sel]
washer *(for tap etc)* un joint [jwān]
wasp une guêpe [gaip]
watch *(wrist-)* une montre [mōntr]
  my watch is slow/fast ma montre retarde/avance [. . . rer-tahrd, ah-vōns]
  will you watch my bags for me? est-ce que vous pouvez surveiller mes bagages? [. . . soor-vay-yay may bah-gahj]
  watch out! attention! [ahtōns-yon]
  watch strap un bracelet de montre [brahs-lay]
water l'eau [oh]
  can I have some water? est-ce que je peux avoir de l'eau?
  hot and cold running water eau courante chaude et froide [oh koo-rōnt shohd ay frwad]
  waterproof imperméable [ānpair-may-ahbl]
  waterskiing le ski nautique [skee noh-teek]
way: the French way à la française [ah lah frōn-sayz]

could you tell me the way to . . .? quel est le chemin
pour aller à . . .? [kel ay ler sher-mān poor ah-lay ah]
YOU MAY THEN HEAR . . .

tournez . . ., prenez . . . *turn . . ., go . . .*
à droite *right*, à gauche *left*
continuez tout droit *keep straight on*
aux feux *at the lights*

we nous [noo]

weak faible [faibl]

weather le temps [tōn]

what's the weather like in . . .? quel temps est-ce
qu'il fait à . . .? [kel tōn eskeel fay ah]

what's the weather forecast? quelles sont les
prévisions de la météo [. . . lay prayveez-yōn der lah
maytay-oh]

YOU MAY THEN HEAR . . .

couvert *overcast,* du soleil *sunny,* de la neige *snow,* de la
pluie *rain,* du vent *wind,* (très) froid *(very) cold,* (très)
chaud *(very) warm*

wedding un mariage [mahr-yahj]

Wednesday mercredi [mairkrer-dee]

week une semaine [ser-men]

a week today dans huit jours [dōn wee joor]

a week tomorrow/on Monday demain/lundi en
huit [der-mān, lān-dee ōn weet]

at the weekend le weekend [wee-kend]

weigh: can you weigh this for me? est-ce que vous
pouvez me peser ça? [. . . mer per-zay sah]

weight le poids [pwah]

well: I'm not feeling well je ne me sens pas très bien
[jer ner mer sōn pah tray bee-yān]

he's not well il ne va pas bien [eel ner vah pah
bee-yān]

very well thanks très bien, merci [tray bee-
yān mair-see]

wellingtons des bottes de caoutchouc [bot der
kahoo-tshoo]

Welsh gallois [gal-wah]

west l'ouest [oo-est]

West Indies les Antilles [ōn-tee]

wet mouillé [moo-yay]; *(weather)* humide [oo-meed]

wet suit combinaison de plongée [kōnbee-
nay-zōn der plōn-jay]

what quel (quelle) [kel]
  what is that? qu'est-ce que c'est? [kesker say]
  what for? pourquoi? [poor-kwah]
  what's that in French? comment est-ce que ça se dit
  en français? [koh-mont esker sah ser dee on fron-say]
wheel une roue [roo]
when quand [kon]
  when is breakfast? à quelle heure est le petit
  déjeuner? [ah kel err . . .]
where où [oo]
  where is . . .? où est . . .? [oo ay]
  where is it? où est-ce que c'est? [wesker say]
  where can we . . .? où est-ce qu'on peut . . .?
  YOU MAY THEN HEAR . . .
  près d'ici *nearby*
  près de . . . *close to* . . .
  très loin *very far*
which quel (quelle) [kel]
  which one? lequel (laquelle)? [ler-kel, lah-kel]
  YOU MAY THEN HEAR . . .
  celui-ci *this one,* celui-là *that one*
whisky un whisky
white blanc [blon]
Whitsun la Pentecôte [pont-koht]
who qui [kee]
wholesale price le prix de gros [pree der groh]
whose: whose is this? à qui est ceci? [ah kee . . .]
why pourquoi [poor-kwah]
  why not? pourquoi pas?
  YOU MAY HEAR . . .
  parce que . . . *because* . . .
wide large [lahrj]
width la largeur [lahr-jerr]
wife: my wife ma femme [fam]
will: will you do it? est-ce que vous pouvez le faire?
  [esker voo poo-vay ler fair]
  I will come back je reviendrai [rerv-yan-dray] *NB:*
  here is the French future tense with the verb 'prendre': je
  prendrai, il prendra, nous prendrons, vous prendrez, ils
  prendront; with 'parler': je parlerai etc
win gagner [gahn-yay]
  who won? qui a gagné? [kee ah gahn-yay]
wind le vent [von]

window la fenêtre [fer-naitr]
  (of car) la vitre [veetr]
  it's in the window c'est dans la vitrine [say dōn lah
  vee-treen]
windscreen le pare-brise [par-breez]
  windscreen wipers les essuie-glace
  [ay-swee glahs]
windy: it's too windy il y a trop de vent [eelyah troh
  der vōn]
wine du vin [vān]
  wine list la carte des vins [kart day vān]
  red wine du vin rouge [. . . rooj]
  white wine du vin blanc [. . . blōn]
» *TRAVEL TIP: enjoy the simpler 'vins de table' or 'vins de
  pays': they are generally good quality and cheap*
winter l'hiver [ee-vair]
wire du fil métallique [feel maytah-leek]
  (electrical) un fil électrique [. . . aylek-treek]
wish: best wishes meilleurs voeux [may-yerr ver]
  (on letter) meilleures pensées [. . . pōn-say]
with avec [ah-vek]
without sans [sōn]
witness un témoin [tay-mwān]
  will you act as witness for me? est-ce que vous
  pouvez me servir de témoin? [. . . mer sair-veer . . .]
woman une femme [fam]
wonderful magnifique [mahnee-feek]
wood du bois [bwah]
  (forest) un bois
wool de la laine [len]
word un mot [moh]
  I don't know that word je ne connais pas ce mot [jer
  ner koh-nay pah ser moh]
work travailler [travah-yay]
  it's not working ça ne marche pas [sah ner marsh
  pah]
  how does it work? comment ça marche?
  I work in London je travaille à Londres
  [jer trah-vie . . .]
worn out usé [oo-zay]
worry les soucis [soo-see]
  don't worry ne vous inquiétez pas [ner vooz
  ānk-yay-tay pah]

I'm worried about ... je suis inquiet pour ... [jer swee ānk-yay poor]

worse: it's worse c'est pire [say peer]

he's getting worse son état s'aggrave [sōn ay-tah sah-grahv]

the worst le pire

worth: it's not worth that much ça ne vaut pas autant [sah ner voh pah oh-tōn]

is it worthwhile going to ...? est-ce que ça vaut la peine d'aller à ...?
[esker sah voh lah pen dah-lay ah]

50F worth of petrol pour cinquante francs d'essence [poor ...]

wrap: could you wrap it up? est-ce que vous pouvez me l'envelopper? [. . . mer lōnv-loh-pay]

wrench une clé anglaise [klay ōn-glayz]

wrist le poignet [pwahn-yay]

write écrire [ay-kreer]

could you write it down? est-ce que vous pouvez me l'écrire?

I'll write to you je vous écrirai
[jer vooz aykree-ray]

writing paper du papier à lettres
[pahp-yay ah laitr]

wrong: I think the bill's wrong je crois qu'il y a une erreur dans l'addition [jer krwah keel yah oon ay-rerr dōn lahdees-yōn]

there's something wrong with ... il y a quelque chose qui ne va pas dans ... [eelyah kelker-shoz kee ne vah pah dōn]

sorry, wrong number! excusez-moi, j'ai fait un faux numéro
[exkoo-zay mwah jay fay ān foh noomay-roh]

you are wrong vous vous trompez
[voo voo trōn-pay]

X-ray une radio [rahd-yoh]

yacht un yacht [yot]

yard

» *TRAVEL TIP: 1 yard = 91.44 cm = 0.91 m*

year une année [ah-nay]

this year cette année

next year l'année prochaine [... proh-shain]

yellow jaune [jon]

yes oui [wee]

yesterday hier [yair]

   the day before yesterday avant-hier [ahvont-yair]

   yesterday morning/afternoon hier matin/après-midi [. . . mah-tān, ahpray-mee-dee]

yet: is it ready yet? est-ce que c'est déjà prêt? [esker say day-jah pray]

   not yet pas encore [pahz ōn-kor]

yoghurt un yaourt [yah-oort]

you vous [voo]

» *TRAVEL TIP: we have systematically given the more formal 'you' form in this book: the 'vous' form; with friends or young people, you can use the less formal 'tu' form, which sounds the same as the 'je' form: 'je veux', 'tu veux'; for 'your', the less formal form is 'ton, ta, tes'*

young jeune [jern]

your votre, vos [vohtr, voh]

   your car/son votre voiture/fils

   your tickets/cars vos billets/voitures

   it's yours c'est le (la) vôtre

   these are yours ce sont les vôtres [ser sōn lay vohtr]

   see **you**

Youth Hostel une auberge de jeunesse [oh-bairj der jer-nes]

» *TRAVEL TIP: you will be asked to produce your YHA card and passport*

zero zéro [zay-roh]

   below zero en dessous de zéro [ōn der-soo . . .]

zip une fermeture éclair [fairmer-toor ay-klair]

zone bleue *area where you can only park for a limited period and must display a parking disc (enquire at the 'syndicat d'initiative')*

zoo le zoo [zoh]

....

1 un [ān]	7 sept [set]
2 deux [der]	8 huit [weet]
3 trois [trwah]	9 neuf [nerf]
4 quatre [kahtr]	10 dix [dees]
5 cinq [sānk]	11 onze [ōnz]
6 six [sees]	12 douze [dooz]

13 treize [trayz]	17 dix-sept [dee-set]
14 quatorze [kah-torz]	18 dix-huit [deez-weet]
15 quinze [kānz]	19 dix-neuf [deez-nerf]
16 seize [sayz]	20 vingt [vānt]
21 vingt-et-un [vān-tay-ān]	
22 vingt-deux [vānt-der]	
23 vingt-trois [vānt-trwah]	

30 trente [trōnt]	50 cinquante [sān-kōnt]
40 quarante [kah-rōnt]	60 soixante [swah-sōnt]

70 soixante-dix [swah-sōnt-dees]
71 soixante et onze [swah-sōnt ay ōnz]
72 soixante-douze [swah-sōnt dooz]
» *TRAVEL TIP: in Switzerland and Belgium, 'septante'*
[sep-tont], *'septante et un' etc*
80 quatre-vingts [kahtrer-vān]
81 quatre-vingt un [. . . ān]
90 quatre-vingt-dix [kahtrer-vān-dees]
91 quatre-vingt-onze [. . . ōnz]
» *TRAVEL TIP: in Switzerland and Belgium, 'nonante'*
[ner-nont], *'nonante et un' etc*

100 cent [sōn], 101 cent un [sōn ān]
200 deux cents, 285 deux cent quatre-vingt cinq
1000 mille [meel], 2300 deux mille trois cent
1 000 000 un million [mee-yōn], 0 zéro [zay-roh]
0.5 zéro virgule [veer-gool] cinq, 0,5

1st premier [prerm-yay], 2nd deuxième [derz-yem]
3rd troisième [trwahz-yem], 21st vingt-et-unième
[. . . ay-oon-yem], *etc (see also* **date**)

» *TRAVEL TIP: telephone numbers are read out as two- or three-figure numbers: 220450 is 22/04/50 (vingt-deux/ zéro quatre/cinquante); 2240098 is 224/00/98 (deux cent vingt-quatre/zéro zéro/ quatre-vingt-dix-huit)*

Escape the

VOLCANO

W10

Stephanie Dagg

MENTOR
BOOKS

This Edition first published 1998 by

MENTOR BOOKS
43 Furze Road,
Sandyford Industrial Estate,
Dublin 18.

Tel. + 353 1 295 2112/3   Fax. + 353 1 295 2114

ISBN: 1-902586-02-6

Cover Illustration: Nicola Sedgwick
Typesetting, editing, design and layout by Mentor Books

Printed in Ireland by ColourBooks

3 5 7 9 10 8 6 4 2